Becker

**Frommer's™**

# Banff & the Canadian Rockies
# day BY day™

## 1st Edition

## by Christie Pashby

**WILEY**

John Wiley & Sons Canada, Ltd.

# Contents

Published by:

# John Wiley & Sons Canada, Ltd.

6045 Freemont Blvd.
Mississauga, ON L5R 4J3

ISBN 978-0-470-73628-9

Editor: Gene Shannon
Production Editor: Pauline Ricablanca
Project Coordinator: Lynsey Stanford
Editorial Assistant: Katie Wolsley
Photo Editor: Photo Affairs, Inc.
Cartographer: Lohnes+Wright
Vice President, Publishing Services: Karen Bryan
Production by Wiley Indianapolis Composition Services

For information on our other products and services or to obtain technical support, please contact our Customer Care Department within the U.S. at 877/762-2974, outside the U.S. at 317/572-3993 or fax 317/572-4002.

Wiley also publishes its books in a variety of electronic formats. Some content that appears in print may not be available in electronic formats.

Manufactured in China

1   2   3   4   5   RRD   14   13   12   11   10

# A Note from the Editorial Director

Organizing your time. That's what this guide is all about.

Other guides give you long lists of things to see and do and then expect you to fit the pieces together. The Day by Day guides are different. These guides tell you the best of everything, and then they show you how to see it *in the smartest, most time-efficient way*. Our authors have designed detailed itineraries organized by time, neighborhood, or special interest. And each tour comes with a bulleted map that takes you from stop to stop.

Hoping to spot animals in the wild or hike through beautiful alpine meadows? Planning to stay in an authentic mountain lodge or soak in an outdoor hot springs? Whatever your interest or schedule, the Day by Days give you the smartest routes to follow. Not only do we take you to the top attractions, hotels, and restaurants, but we also help you access those special moments that locals get to experience—those "finds" that turn tourists into travelers.

The Day by Days are also your top choice if you're looking for one complete guide for all your travel needs. The best hotels and restaurants for every budget, the greatest shopping values, the wildest nightlife—it's all here.

Why should you trust our judgment? Because our authors personally visit each place they write about. They're an independent lot who say what they think and would never include places they wouldn't recommend to their best friends. They're also open to suggestions from readers. If you'd like to contact them, please send your comments our way at feedback@frommers.com, and we'll pass them on.

Enjoy your Day by Day guide—the most helpful travel companion you can buy. And have the trip of a lifetime.

Warm regards,

*Kelly Regan*

Kelly Regan, Editorial Director
Frommer's Travel Guides

# About the Author

**Christie Pashby** has written for Frommer's for nearly a decade, contributing to titles including *Frommer's Argentina, Frommer's Chile,* and *Frommer's Best Hiking Trips in British Columbia.* She divides her time between the Canadian Rockies and Bariloche, Argentina. A freelance journalist and translator, she also somehow finds the time to run a small guiding business with her husband, and cram in two ski seasons a year. Her website is www.patagonialiving.com.

# Acknowledgments

I'd like to thank my congenial editor Gene Shannon, as well as the staff at Travel Alberta and the Banff Lake Louise Tourism Bureau.

# An Additional Note

Please be advised that travel information is subject to change at any time—and this is especially true of prices. We therefore suggest that you write or call ahead for confirmation when making your travel plans. The authors, editors, and publisher cannot be held responsible for the experiences of readers while traveling. Your safety is important to us, however, so we encourage you to stay alert and be aware of your surroundings.

# Star Ratings, Icons & Abbreviations

Every hotel, restaurant, and attraction listing in this guide has been ranked for quality, value, service, amenities, and special features using a **star-rating system.** Hotels, restaurants, attractions, shopping, and nightlife are rated on a scale of zero stars (recommended) to three stars (exceptional). In addition to the star-rating system, we also use a **kids** icon to point out the best bets for families. Within each tour, we recommend cafes, bars, or restaurants where you can take a break. Each of these stops appears in a shaded box marked with a coffee-cup-shaped bullet ☕.

The following **abbreviations** are used for credit cards:

| | | | | | |
|---|---|---|---|---|---|
| **AE** | American Express | **DISC** | Discover | **V** | Visa |
| **DC** | Diners Club | **MC** | MasterCard | | |

# Travel Resources at Frommers.com

Frommer's travel resources don't end with this guide. **Frommers.com** has travel information on more than 4,000 destinations. We update features regularly, giving you access to the most current trip-planning information and the best airfare, lodging, and car-rental bargains. You can also listen to podcasts, connect with other Frommers.com members through our active-reader forums, share your travel photos, read blogs from guidebook editors and fellow travelers, and much more.

# A Note on Prices

In the "Take a Break" and "Best Bets" sections of this book, we have used a system of dollar signs to show a range of costs for 1 night in a hotel (the price of a double-occupancy room) or the cost of an entree at a restaurant. Use the following table to decipher the dollar signs:

| Cost | Hotels | Restaurants |
|---|---|---|
| $ | under $100 | under $10 |
| $$ | $100–$200 | $10–$20 |
| $$$ | $200–$300 | $20–$30 |
| $$$$ | $300–$400 | $30–$40 |
| $$$$$ | over $400 | over $40 |

# How to Contact Us

In researching this book, we discovered many wonderful places—hotels, restaurants, shops, and more. We're sure you'll find others. Please tell us about them, so we can share the information with your fellow travelers in upcoming editions. If you were disappointed with a recommendation, we'd love to know that, too. Please write to:

*Frommer's Banff & the Canadian Rockies Day by Day,* 1st Edition
John Wiley & Sons Canada, Ltd. • 6045 Freemont Blvd. • Mississauga, ON
L5R 4J3

# 18 Favorite
**Moments**

# 18 Favorite **Moments**

**Legend:**
- Gasoline
- Hospital/First Aid
- (i) Information
- ▲ Mountain
- Point of Interest
- Skiing

0 ___ 10 mi
0 ___ 10 km

1. Gazing at the peaks from the top of Sulphur Mountain
2. Skiing the Great Divide at Sunshine Village
3. Fly fishing on the Upper Bow River
4. Exploring an ice castle on a starry winter's night
5. Catching live jazz at the Banff Centre
6. Skating on a frozen lake
7. Hiking or cross-country skiing into Skoki Lodge
8. Hiking Lake O'Hara Alpine Circuit
9. Viewing Saskatchewan Glacier from Parker Ridge
10. Sunday brunch at the Fairmont Banff Springs
11. Soaking in the Banff Upper Hot Springs on a winter evening
12. Tea at the Plain of the Six Glaciers
13. Wildflowers at Healy Pass
14. Morning coffee run
15. Catching your first wildlife sighting
16. Setting up a mountain picnic
17. Driving the astonishing Icefields Parkway
18. Canoeing on an alpine lake

*Previous page: A hiker admires the scenery along the Lake O'Hara Alpine Circuit.*

**B**anff has been drawing visitors to the Canadian Rocky Mountains for more than a century. They're drawn primarily to nature and the peace of the wilderness. It's not necessarily hip (although Banff has trendy restaurants), and it's certainly nothing new. Banff is dependable yet surprising, a place to stretch yourself physically and reward yourself mentally. The following are some of my favorite experiences in Canada's premier mountain wilderness.

**❶ Gazing at the peaks from the top of Sulphur Mountain.** It's the easiest summit in the Canadian Rockies. Take the 8-minute gondola ride to the top of Sulphur Mountain, then walk the elevated 1km (2/3-mile) boardwalk to Sanson Peak, a truly jaw-dropping lookout. Six mountain ranges are displayed beneath you. Also great for families, this is an easy way to accomplish a kid's first Rocky Mountain summit. Hardcore hikers can hike up the 5.3km (3.3-mile) switchback trail, and then reward their knees by riding the gondola down. *See p 12, bullet ❷.*

**❷ Skiing the Great Divide at Sunshine Village.** On a perfect winter day, catch the Continental Divide chair up to the top of Lookout Mountain, crossing from Alberta into British Columbia en route. The view of Mount Assiniboine, the "Matterhorn of the Rockies," is magnificent, and when the powder is fresh and the sun is shining, your ski back down will be even more thrilling. *See p 43, bullet ❿.*

**❸ Fly fishing on the Upper Bow River.** Slow things down by heading downriver from the Town of Banff on the clear and pristine Upper Bow to try your luck at hooking a brown, brook, or rainbow trout. Remember, it's strictly catch and release, and you must have a permit from Parks Canada. In Jasper, the trout gather on the Maligne River. Since the best fishing often happens on the lousiest days, this is a great rainy-day outing. *See p 153.*

**❹ Exploring an ice castle on a starry winter's night.** Late January brings the annual Ice Magic event to the frozen shores of Lake Louise.

*Sulphur Mountain's peak can be accessed easily by gondola or vigorously on foot.*

*Fly fishing on the Upper Bow River.*

Under the dark sky and beneath the icy glaciers of Mount Victoria, carvers from around the world craft magical creations, culminating with a frozen castle that stays on the lake as long as the lake is frozen. Rent some skates at the Fairmont Chateau Lake Louise, snuggle by the outdoor fire, and sip hot chocolate—the ingredients of a mid-winter's dream come true. *See p 42, bullet* ③.

⑤ **Catching live jazz at the Banff Centre.** Year-round concerts at this globally-renowned arts and cultural center bring in some of the sharpest musicians from around the world. During the summer, the Banff Summer Arts Festival also showcases dance, opera, theater, and literary journalism. An inspiring way to spend the evening! *See p 55, bullet* ⑯.

⑥ **Skating on a frozen lake.** Clear as glass on a crisp winter day, the shallow Vermillion Lakes, close to the Town of Banff, make for a magical ice rink. The crisp mountain views and glimpses of fish wintering below the ice add to the icy drama. What could be more Canadian? Just be sure to check ice thickness with Parks Canada first. In Jasper, try Pyramid Lake. *See p 41, bullet* ③.

⑦ **Hiking or cross-country skiing into Skoki Lodge.** This historic cabin tucked in the woods behind Lake Louise Ski Resort may be the place that defined rustic mountain charm. The 11km (6.8-mile) trail leads to a wooden cabin with private rooms, home cooking, endless trails—and no electricity or running water. It's like stepping back in time to a pure and unspoiled mountain retreat. *See p 82.*

⑧ **Hiking Lake O'Hara Alpine Circuit.** Just the word "O'Hara" brings oohs and aahs from veteran hikers. Across the British Columbia border behind Lake Louise, in Yoho National Park, this is an exquisite hiking destination, dotted with meadows, lookouts, ridge-walks, turquoise lakes, and meticulously chiselled stone trails. There are a half-dozen superb hikes to choose from, but the Alpine Circuit highlights the best of the best. Remember to book your bus ride up to the lake in advance. *See p 26.*

⑨ **Viewing Saskatchewan Glacier from Parker Ridge.** Hike for just over an hour for views even more stunning than those you can see from your car on the Icefields Parkway. The trail starts steeply, but soon plateaus out into the subalpine zone, offering gorgeous views of the Saskatchewan Glacier and Mount Athabasca. Don't forget to look down and around you too—you may see fossils, rosy finches, mountain goats, and maybe even a grizzly bear. For solitude and spectacular vistas, few short hikes in the world can compare. *See p 46, bullet* ⑦.

⑩ **Sunday brunch at the Fairmont Banff Springs.** In the stately Bow Valley Grill inside this legendary hotel, you can sample a stellar array of gourmet Canadiana, from smoked Wild Pacific salmon and free-range eggs Benedict, to roasted Alberta beef and maple brownies. Ask for a window table for views of Fairholme Range and Bow River, and bring your appetite. Reservations recommended. *See p 14, bullet* ③.

**⑪ Soaking in the Banff Upper Hot Springs on a winter evening.** If it's cold and you've been skiing all day, you're in the right town—just head to the historic bathhouse to relax in the natural hot pools (ranging from 99°–104°F/37°–40°C), open until 10pm weeknights in winter and 11pm on winter weekends. Other hot springs in the mountain parks worth visiting include Miette Hot Springs in Jasper National Park and the Radium Hot Springs in Kootenay National Park. *See p 14, bullet ⑦*.

**⑫ Tea at the Plain of the Six Glaciers.** Drawing hikers since 1924, this historic tea house is a rustic cabin nestled in a gorgeous location at the back of Lake Louise. It's a 2-hour hike to get here—surely you deserve a piece of chocolate cake or banana loaf? Take your pot of tea and sit outside to marvel at the six glaciers that cling to Aberdeen, Lefroy, Victoria, and Popes Peak. *See p 146.*

**⑬ Wildflowers at Healy Pass.** In the high alpine zone, hardy wildflowers like moss Campion, purple Saxifrage, glacier lilies, and alpine forget-me-nots bloom into gorgeous colors from mid-July to mid-August. This pass just beside Sunshine Village ski area is one of the finest areas for these brilliant displays. Hike the 12km (7.5-mile) trail up to alpine meadows, or cheat by taking the Sunshine Meadows shuttle up most of the way. In Jasper, head to Mount Edith Cavell. *See p 27, bullet ④*.

**⑭ Morning coffee run.** Early morning is the quietest time of the day on the otherwise-bustling main strip of Banff Avenue. Before 9am, it's the peaceful terrain of locals. Join them for a cafe latte and whole wheat waffles (served with apple maple sauce) at the Wild Flour Bakery. As the workers head off, relish your vacation time with a stroll along the Bow River. In Jasper, do the same at the Bear's Paw Bakery. *See p 127.*

**⑮ Catching your first wildlife sighting.** Whether it's an elk munching on grass on a lawn or a grizzly bear crossing an avalanche path, each glimpse of a wild animal in Banff is a gift. There are no guarantees, but there's a good chance that

*The crystal clear surface of Lake O'Hara in Yoho National Park.*

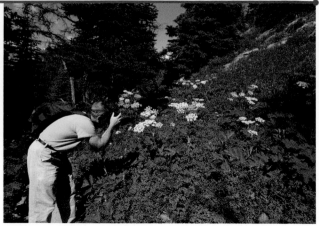

*The alpine wildflowers at Healy Pass are picture-perfect in July and August.*

you'll see bighorn sheep at Lake Minnewanka at dusk or dawn. Some animals, of course, require more seriousness than others. Visit the Parks Canada Visitors Centres for more information. *See p 13, bullet* ❶.

**⑯ Setting up a mountain picnic.** Quieter than the Trans-Canada Highway, the Bow Valley Parkway's best picnic spot is at the Storm Mount Lookout, just north of Castle Junction, for great views and photo-ops. Pick up supplies for a scrumptious picnic at the Bison Bistro's General Store in Banff or at Laggan's in Lake Louise. *See p 142.*

**⑰ Driving the astonishing Ice-fields Parkway.** For 230km (143 miles), drive a road that feels like it's been carved inside the earth, with massive mountains clinging to the Continental Divide, ancient glaciers, and ragged peaks. At the middle are the Columbia Icefields, the liquid heart from which the waters of the nation pump. Oh, and there are mountain goats and grizzly bears too! *See p 64.*

**⑱ Canoeing on an alpine lake.** Emerald, Maligne, Moraine . . . their names simply invite you to grab a paddle and launch a canoe upon their sublime shores. Out alone (or with a friend) on a placid alpine lake, with your reflection blending with that of giant rocky peaks on the ripples beside you, you'll find you're living inside your own postcard from paradise. Moraine Lake is next to Lake Louise and is less visited but still easy to access, making it my top choice. *See p 63, bullet* ❾. ●

*Canoeing on a serene alpine lake.*

# 1

# Strategies for Seeing **Banff & the Canadian Rockies**

# Banff & the Canadian Rockies

The beautiful Canadian Rockies are a vast area with so much to see and do. Your time is precious and you need to plan according to the seasons, the length of your visit, and your goals and tastes. Don't try to do it all—the magic in Banff is in the quietest moments. In this chapter I have several tips to help you make the most of your time.

### Rule #1: Get out of town!
While the Town of Banff holds most of the lodgings and restaurants, not to mention shops and nightlife, it's what you'll find in the rest of the park that will most astound you. Those particularly interested in solitude should head to a nearby national park—Jasper in the north, or Kootenay and Yoho to the west—or to one of the many backcountry lodges dotted throughout the park. Even day trips in a car or a short hike count towards spreading your wings here.

### Rule #2: Go to the experts and visit the Parks Canada Information Centres
These should be your first stop, whether it's in the Town of Banff, at Lake Louise, or in Jasper. Pick up maps and permits and take in interpretive exhibits that will greatly enhance your experience in the Canadian Rockies. The friendly staff members have the latest trail, road, avalanche, and wildlife reports, and can answer just about any question you have.

### Rule #3: Don't over-schedule
Jam-packing your days from an early-morning bird-watching trip to a late-night stargazing excursion will only leave you exhausted. The loveliest moments in Banff are those that surprise you—spotting a wolf on a quiet road, or having a leisurely picnic by the river. Give yourself time for spontaneous adventure and explorations.

### Rule #4: Allow plenty of travel time
Not only are the distances great, but you'll find lots of mountains along the way that provide twists and turns—there are few straight lines in the Canadian Rockies. And along the way from A to B, there'll likely be dozens of photo opportunities and maybe even some wildlife sightings. Plan to get out of the car often, and take your time while driving.

### Rule #5: Come in the shoulder season
Not only will it save you money, but you'll avoid the crowds. June is considered off-season, and September (my favorite month in Banff) is great for hiking. For winter travelers, try pre-Christmas December for good deals and April for spring skiing.

### Rule #6: Be prepared for weather
In the Rockies, it's common to see all four seasons in a day, any time of the year. Even in the middle of summer, don't be surprised to see snow—bring appropriate clothing and never hit the trail without a good jacket, sunscreen, and a bottle of water.

*The Lake Louise visitor centre provides maps, permits, and park information.*

*Mountains at every turn can make for winding roads and slow driving.*

### Rule #7: Try something new

Banff is a great place to do something you've never done before—or something you haven't done in years. Hiking isn't just for the super-fit and horseback riding ain't only for cowboys. The campground up at Lake O'Hara may be the most accessible backcountry camping in the mountains, so give it a try. In wintertime, take a snowboard lesson or try ice skating. Vacations are for breaking free!

*Care-free skiing in the off-season.*

### Rule #8: Pick one central activity each day, then plan around it

Some low-key days will be for relaxing and strolling Banff Avenue. Others, like when you're heading out for a hike, require you to plan ahead—get your lunch the day before, check trail and weather conditions, bring lots of water, and get a good night's sleep. Be logical so that you don't have to back-track.

### Rule #9: Think outside the park

Save cash by staying in a hotel just outside Banff. The Town of Canmore, just 20km (12 miles)—a 15-min. drive—east of Banff, is a lovely mountain town with an impressive list of affordable hotel options.

### Rule #10: Use this book as a reference, not a concrete plan

Don't worry; I won't be hurt if you don't follow every single tour I lay out here. Read through the options I present, pick the ones that most appeal to you, and adapt them to your personal circumstances. ●

# 2 The Best Full-Day Tours

# Banff **in Three Days**

**DAY 1**
1 Banff Information Centre
2 Sulphur Mountain Gondola
3 Fairmont Banff Springs Hotel
4 Coyotes Grill
5 Tunnel Mountain
6 Bison Mountain Bistro
7 Upper Hot Springs

**DAY 2**
8 Lake Louise Village
9 Laggan's Mountain Deli
10 Lake Louise
11 Fairmont Chateau
    Lake Louise
12 Tea at the Chateau
13 Moraine Lake
14 Bow Valley Parkway

**DAY 3**
15 Crowfoot Glacier
16 Peyto Lake
17 Saskatchewan Crossing
18 Columbia Icefields
19 Columbia Glacial
    Icefields Experience

To Jasper National Park

LYELL ICEFIELD

Park Gate

Saskatchewan Crossing

Siffleur Wilderness

FRESHFIELD ICEFIELD

WAPTA ICEFIELD

Icefields Parkway

BANFF NATIONAL PARK

Red Deer River

Bow River

Kicking Horse Pass

Lake Louise Village

Field

TEMPLE MTN.

CASTLE MTN.

CASCADE MTN.

Castle Junction

Johnston Canyon

KOOTENAY NATIONAL PARK

Banff

Area of inset

MT. RUNDLE

ALBERTA
BRITISH COLUMBIA

Park Gate

Radium Hot Springs

Edmonton

ALBERTA

BRITISH COLUMBIA

Jasper

Golden

Lake Louise

Calgary

Banff

Area of map

CANADA
UNITED STATES

Wolf

Bear

Caribou

Otter

Bow River

Spray Av.

Tunnel Mountain Dr.

St. Julien Rd.

Mountain Av.

Spray River

**Banff**

| | Gasoline |
| i | Information |
| ▲ | Mountain |
| ■ | Point of Interest |
| ⚡ | Skiing |

*Previous page: The Rocky Mountaineer traveling along the Canadian Pacific Railway.*

**L**ocated at the confluence of the Spray and Bow rivers, and on the lower slopes of Tunnel and Sulphur mountains, the Town of Banff is rich in culture and history, with adventure at your doorstep. START: **Banff Info Centre, corner of Wolf St. and Bear St. Trip Length: 7km + 4.6km hike is 11.6km (7.2 miles).**

## Travel Tip

Avoid parking hassles by using the ROAM hybrid bus system, which runs down all the routes mentioned below. An unlimited day pass costs $5. For more information call ☎ 403/762-6770. Days 2 and 3 require your own vehicle.

### Day 1

**1** ★★ **Banff Information Centre.** No visit to Banff should start anywhere else. Stock up on maps and free self-guided tour brochures, and get helpful advice from the knowledgeable and friendly staff of the Parks Canada, Banff/Lake Louise Tourism Bureau, and Friends of Banff desks. See p 51. ⏱ *30 min. 224 Banff Ave. ☎ 403/762-1550. Late Sept to mid-May 9am–5pm; May 15–June 17 and Sept 10–23 9am–7pm; June 18–Sept 9 8am–8pm.*

Hop on the ROAM bus 1 or drive up Banff Avenue over the Bow

*The staff at the Banff Information Centre are knowledgeable and eager to help.*

*The Sulphur Mountain Gondola.*

River Bridge. Take a left after the bridge onto Spray Avenue and a quick right up Mountain Road until you arrive at:

**2** ★ kids **Sulphur Mountain Gondola.** A quick 7-minute gondola ride takes you to the top of this 2,285m (7,496 ft.) peak. Walk the elevated boardwalk to Sanson Peak. Bring a sweater! ⏱ *60 min. At the end of Mountain Rd., 2.5km (1½ miles) from Banff Ave. ☎ 403/762-2523. Adults $19, kids 6 and up $14. Kids under 6 free. Jan 1–4, Jan 17–30, and Nov 30–Dec 31 daily 10am–4pm; Jan 5–16 closed for annual maintenance; Jan 31–Apr 3 daily 10am–5pm; Apr 4–May 29 daily 8:30am–6pm; May 30–Aug 23 daily 8:30am–9pm; Aug 24–Sep 6 daily 8:30am–8pm; Sep 7–Oct 12 daily 8:30am–6:30pm; Oct 13–Nov 29 daily 8:30am–4:30pm.*

Head back down Mountain Road, taking a right at Spray Avenue. If you are on the ROAM bus 1, you'll have to change lines to bus

2 at the corner of Spray Avenue and Mountain Road. Continue to the right until you arrive at:

**❸ ★★ Fairmont Banff Springs Hotel.** Even if all you do is drive by, you can't miss the unmistakable stone towers and green roof of this national landmark. Ostentatious and oozing with amenities, it's an expensive place to stay (see p 79), but a marvelous building and certainly a must-see on any trip to Banff. Non-guests are welcome to grab a meal or take a short tour of the hotel. ⏲ *45 min. 405 Spray Ave.* ☎ *403/762-2211.*

From the Banff Springs, head back down Banff Avenue into town. Turn left on Caribou Street to:

**❹ Lunch at Coyotes Grill.** Few places have stood the test of time as well as this Southwest-inspired bistro in the heart of Banff. Run by devoted locals, the food is fresh and tasty. Try a corn-crusted pizza or chicken enchilada. *206 Caribou St.* ☎ *403/762-3963. $$*

Leave the streets behind, walking up Wolf Street towards the Banff Centre, keeping an eye out for the trail head for:

**❺ ★★ Tunnel Mountain Hike.** Work off lunch by hiking this classic Banff trail (see p 14) that heads right out of the heart of town. It's a 2.3km (1.4-mile) hike that takes you 300m (984 ft.) up to the lookout. One of the oldest trails in the park, this is very popular with Banff locals. ⏲ *2.5 hr. Trail head is at St. Julien Rd., 300m (984 ft.) uphill from the Wolf St. junction.*

Head back into town on Wolf Street, turning left on Bear Street. Half a block down, you'll find:

**❻ Bison Mountain Bistro.** Hit the sunny patio here for a treat. Overlooking Bear Street and Mount Rundle, it's got the best view of any patio in town. Upscale cheese and meat trays make great appetizers, and there's a long wine-by-the-glass menu and local beers on tap. *See p 70. 211 Bear St.* ☎ *403/762-5550. $$*

After a leisurely meal, hop back on the ROAM bus 1 or drive up Mountain Road towards:

**❼ ★★ Upper Hot Springs.** For more than a century, visitors have come to Banff to "take the waters." Evenings are the best time at these historic pools. ⏲ *60 min. At the end of Mountain Rd., 2.5km (1½ miles) from downtown Banff.* ☎ *403/762-1515. Sept 9–May 14 Sun–Thurs 10am–10pm and Fri–Sat 10am–11pm; May 15–Sept 13 daily 9am–11pm. Adult $7.30, seniors and children (3–17) $6.30.*

*Non-guests can enjoy the Fairmont Banff Springs Hotel over a meal or short tour.*

## Day 2

You day begins with a delightful 45-minute drive to Lake Louise. Head straight there from Banff—you'll have time later in the afternoon to look around the Bow Valley. Your goal is to beat the crowds to the lake, and to secure the best light for photographing.

**8** ★ **Lake Louise Village.** A small "'hamlet" just off the Trans-Canada Highway, this is a collection of hotels, restaurants, gas stations, and shops, centered at the Samson Mall. Pick up a snack or grab a new fleece if the weather has soured. The Parks Canada Information Centre is just behind the shopping plaza, worth a visit for trail and wildlife updates. 🕐 *40 min. 58km (36 miles) west of Town of Banff on Trans-Canada Hwy. 1.*

**9** **Laggan's Mountain Deli.** This unpretentious coffee and sandwich shop is popular with hikers, bikers, skiers, and anybody on the move. It's in the middle of Samson Mall. Beat the crowds by entering the alternative door on the left side and heading for the second cashier. *101 Lake Louise Dr., in Samson Mall.* ☎ *403/522-2017. $.*

Drive out of the Samson Mall parking lot onto Village Road, turning left at Lake Louise Drive and heading up the hill until you reach:

**10** ★★★ **Lake Louise.** Perhaps the most photographed lake in Canada, this stunner draws thousands of visitors every week from every corner of the globe. At the back of the lake, Mount Victoria and the Victoria Glacier make an imposing backdrop. Take an hour to stroll to the back of the lake. Find a quiet spot for a snack.

*Lake Louise attracts photographers from all around the world.*

It's impossible to miss the massive building to your right:

**11** ★★ **Chateau Lake Louise.** This landmark hotel is known as "'the diamond in the wilderness." For more than 115 years, mountaineers, artists, and lovers of the outdoors have been drawn to the sublime landscape outside of, and the grace inside of, this hotel. 🕐 *30 min. 111 Lake Louise Dr.* ☎ *403/522-1818.*

**12** **Tea at the Chateau.** If you're not a guest, you can experience the refined elegance of this famous hotel by reserving a table for afternoon tea in the Lakeview Lounge. By reservation only. *111 Lake Louise Dr.* ☎ *403/522-1818. $$*

Drive out of the parking lot and take the first right on the Moraine Lake Road, which leads you to:

**13** ★★★ **Moraine Lake.** Some say Louise's less-visited sister lake is even more beautiful. Wild and dramatic, Moraine Lake is surrounded by 10 spire-like peaks.

*Colorful canoes sit on a dock above Moraine Lake.*

There's a great interpretive trail to the Moraine Lake Rockpile. 🕐 *45 min. 13km (8 miles) south of Lake Louise on Moraine Lake Road.*

Bid farewell to the Lake Louise area, driving back down to the village. Drive over the Trans-Canada Highway, taking the next right on to:

### ⓮ Bow Valley Parkway 1A.

Built in 1920, the first road connecting Banff and Lake Louise still feels more like a mountain road than an expressway. Compared to the Trans-Canada Highway, the Parkway is quieter, and gives you a much better chance for wildlife sightings.

The day ends returning on the Bow Valley Parkway 1A and then finally on the Trans-Canada Highway into the Town of Banff.

### Day 3

One of the most beautiful drives in the entire world, a day on the Icefields is not to be missed. Continuing north on the Icefields Parkway from Lake Louise, the road steadily climbs higher and higher and the views become more and more dramatic as you make your way through three river valleys and pass beneath towering glacier-topped peaks. Get an early start, as the first stop is over an hour from Banff.

### Travel Tip

Food options are next-to-nonexistent once you pass Lake Louise, so pick up a picnic there or in Banff. You must have a valid Park Pass to drive on this highway. See p 58.

### ⓯ ★ Crowfoot Glacier. The first

of a long line-up of glaciers you'll see once resembled the foot of a crow (hence the name), but has shrunk significantly. There are interpretive signs posted at the roadside viewpoint. 🕐 *10 min. 32km (20 miles) from Lake Louise on Hwy. 93, the Icefields Parkway.*

Continue north on the Icefields Parkway to:

### ⓰ ★★ Peyto Lake. There is a

short interpretive trail to this beautifully turquoise gem, named for pioneer guide Bill Peyto, who was also a warden in Banff National Park. 🕐 *20 min. 42km (26 miles)*

*The lookout onto Peyto Lake is a short hike away from Icefields Parkway.*

*Crowfoot Glacier, one of the many breathtaking sights along the Icefields Parkway.*

from Lake Louise on Hwy. 93, the Icefields Pkwy.

Continue north on the Icefields Parkway to:

**⑰ Saskatchewan Crossing.** This is the only place with any kind of services between Lake Louise and the Icefields Centre. Besides lovely views of the Mistaya, Howse, and North Saskatchewan river valleys, there is a warden station, gas station, snack bar, and gift shop. ⏱ *10 min. 50 km (31 miles) from Lake Louise on Hwy. 93, the Icefields Pkwy.*

Continue north on the Icefields Parkway to:

**⑱ ★★★ Columbia Icefields.** Just north of the Banff-Jasper park border, this is an area of glacial ice and snow measuring 190 sq. km (73 sq. miles) that is up to 350m (1,148 ft.) deep in places. It'll give you an idea what the northern part of North America may have looked like during the Earth's last ice age. There are six main glaciers flowing from the Columbia Icefield. Park at the Icefields Centre, the main building in the area. This is where you need to

go to sign up for a tour on the snocoach. ⏱ *2–3 hr. total. 125km (78 miles) from Lake Louise on Hwy. 93, the Icefields Pkwy.* ☎ *780/852-6288. May 1–June 13 and Sept 3–Oct 15 daily 9am–5pm; June 14–Sept 2 daily 9am–6pm; closed Oct 16–Apr 30.*

Directly across the highway is:

**⑲ ★★ kids The Columbia Glacier Icefield Experience.** Take a giant "snocoach" onto the Athabasca Glacier, which drops you off in the middle of the ice where you can walk around. Expect to have to wait for availability in tours, especially in July and August. Come early or late for shorter wait times. Tours leave every 15 minutes or so. ⏱ *90 min.* ☎ *403/762-6700. Adults $49, kids 6–15 $24. Apr 10–30 and Oct 1–18 daily 10am–4pm; May 1–31 and Sept 1–31 daily 9am–5pm; June 1–Aug 31 daily 9am–6pm. 125km (78 miles) from Lake Louise on Hwy. 93, the Icefields Pkwy.*

The day ends retracing your steps back to Banff on Hwy. 93 and then on the Trans-Canada Hwy. 1.

# Best in **One Week**

Gasoline

*i* Information

▲ Mountain

■ Point of Interest

1 Town of Banff
2 Horseback riding at the Spray River
3 Lake Louise
4 Icefields Parkway
5 Hiking at Lake Louise
6 Yoho National Park
  6a Spiral Tunnels
  6b Takakkaw Falls
  6c Field
  6d Chercher Le Vache Café
  6e Emerald Lake
  6f Cilantro on the Lake
7 Biking at Lake Louise

**H**aving a few extra days allows you time to explore the back-country of Banff National Park, and visit the historically—and geo-graphically—fascinating Yoho National Park, next door to Banff. You can blend both active adventures, like hiking and horseback riding, with tra-ditional touring and sightseeing. START: **Town of Banff.**

### Day 1
Follows the Town of Banff tour from Day 1 above.

### Day 2
Saddle up today to head into the mountains. Follow in the steps of cowboys, pack guides, and wilder-ness explorers near Banff. **Holiday on Horseback's** Warner's Stables, which has run trail rides in Banff for nearly 50 years, has a full-day trip that heads up the Spray River and includes a barbecue lunch (see p 154). *132 Banff Ave.* ☎ *800/661-8352 or 403/762-4551.*

### Day 3
Today follows Day 2 of "Banff in 3 Days" with one difference: Drive up to Lake Louise on the Bow Valley Parkway, stopping at Johnston Can-yon and Muleshoe en route (see p 59), and plan on spending the next few nights based out of Lake Louise.

*Trail riding up the Spray River.*

### Day 4
Today follows Day 3 of "Banff in 3 Days," taking in all the highlights of the spectacular Icefields Parkway, returning to Lake Louise in the evening.

### Day 5
Lake Louise hiking: In a land of super-latives, there are many outstanding hiking options to choose from. The classic Lake Louise hike, the Highline Trail, connects Lake Agnes with the Plain of the Six Glaciers, two historic tea houses, massive glaciers, and a lovely, gentle downhill finish. *Tip:* Pick up lunch supplies at Laggan's in Sam-son Mall, and be sure to bring plenty of water! *See Chapter 6 for trail descriptions.*

### Day 6
Yoho National Park: "Yoho" is an expression of awe and wonder in the Cree language, and that's just what you'll experience in this park, located just over the provincial border from Banff in British Columbia. Yoho show-cases the western slopes of the Rockies with dozens of spectacular waterfalls and the Kicking Horse River. It's also an interesting spot for history buffs. START: **Lake Louise.**

Take the Trans-Canada Hwy. 1 west from Lake Louise 9.2km (5¾ miles) to the border between Alberta and British Columbia. 8.7km (5½ miles) west of the bor-der, turn off into the roadside interpretive display at:

**6A ★ Spiral Tunnels.** Steep as it is, the CPR (Canadian Pacific Rail-way) in the 1880s selected the

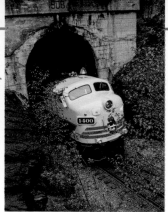

*A train emerging from Cathedral Mountain through the Spiral Tunnels.*

Kicking Horse Pass as the easiest way over the Rockies. But it was still very, very steep, and soon enough trains were crashing down the so-called "Big Hill." The Spiral Tunnels were designed 100 years ago to take trains through two loops inside Cathedral Mountain, easing the grade. View the Spiral Tunnels from the side of Trans-Canada Hwy. 1 just up the hill from Field; there are excellent interpretive signs, and if your timing's good, you'll actually catch a train going through the tunnels (on an average day, 25 to 30

trains pass through the tunnels, though not on a regular schedule).

**Continue down the hill on the Trans-Canada Highway another 3.7km (2¼ miles), turning right at Yoho Valley Road for:**

**6B ★★ Takakkaw Falls.** Reach the fourth-highest waterfall in Canada by driving up the Kicking Horse River on Yoho Valley Road (not recommended for large RVs or trailers). If you love waterfalls, you've come to the right place. Hike in another hour along the Yoho Valley trail past Staircase Falls and Point Lace Falls to see Laughing Falls and then on to beautiful Twin Falls.

**Drive back out to the Trans-Canada Hwy. 1, continuing 1.8km (1 mile) west to the Field turnoff.**

**6C ★ Field.** With a population of only 200 souls, the tiny town of Field, BC has a gorgeous setting beside the Kicking Horse River and beneath Mount Stephen. There are a few charming shops, including the Velvet Antler Pottery. ⏱ *30 min. (on Stephen Ave. next to Chercher La Vache Café, ☎ 250/343-6456). 27km (17 miles) from Lake Louise.*

*Takakkaw Falls in Yoho National Park.*

Head through tiny Field, turning right on Kicking Horse Avenue, and make a quick U-turn at Stephen Avenue to find:

**6D** ★ **Chercher La Vache Café.** A cozy deli in historic Field is a good stop any time of day: pre-hike for a breakfast sandwich or to get a "designer" sandwich to go. Or come by post-hike for a date square, brownie, and cup of tea. It's even open for dinner, with salads, pastas, and a great veggie chili. *318 Stephen Ave., at the corner of Kicking Horse Ave.* ☎ *250/343-6336. www. chercherlavachecafe.com. $$.*

Back out on the Trans-Canada Highway, turn left (west) and continue 2km (1¼ miles) to the turnoff for Emerald Lake Road. Drive 8km (5 miles) until you reach:

**6E** ★★ **Emerald Lake.** Move past the crowded parking lot and hike the lovely 5km (3.1-mile) trail around this marvelous alpine lake. With just a little bit of up and down, this wide trail that circles the pristine Emerald Lake is rich and delightful, almost easy enough to be considered a stroll. Legendary local guide Tom Wilson is credited for having "discovered" this natural marvel in 1882 as part of a route-scouting for the Canadian Pacific Railroad. This is a great family outing or leg-stretcher; it showcases a gem of a lake, and the interpretive signs are informative.

**6F** ★ **Cilantro on the Lake** Open only during the summertime, this is a pretty mountain bistro at Emerald Lake Lodge offering wood-fired flatbread pizzas, gourmet burgers, and micro-brewed beer in a sublimely beautiful setting. Sit on the lovely,

*Diners on the patio at Cilantro on the Lake take in the alpine view.*

sunny patio overlooking Emerald Lake or inside the spectacular timber-frame lodge. *On Emerald Lake Rd., 8km (5 miles) off Trans-Canada Hwy., at a turnoff 2km (1¼ miles) south of Field.* ☎ *250/343-6321. $$*

**Day 7**
Your final day is for some morning adventure. Rent a mountain bike from **Wilson Mountain Sports** in Samson Mall (from $15/hour; ☎ 866/929-3636 or 403/522-2178) and ride the 9km (5.6-mile) return classic Tramline Trail. Families will prefer the gentle Bow River Loop or the Great Divide Bike Path, which is better suited to a road bike. Then give yourself plenty of time to say goodbye to the Rockies and head out.

# Best in **Two Weeks**

DAY 1
**1** Town of Banff

DAY 2
**2** Horseback Riding on the Spray River

DAY 3
**3** Sunshine Meadows

DAY 4
**4** Kootenay National Park

DAY 5
**5** Lake Louise

DAY 6
**6** Hiking in Paradise Valley/ Larch Valley

DAY 7
**7** Yoho National Park

DAY 8
**8** Camping at Lake O'Hara

DAY 9
**9** Hiking at Lake O'Hara

DAY 10
**10** Icefields Parkway

DAY 11
**11** Tour of Jasper Townsite and Area

DAY 12
**12** Maligne Valley

DAY 13
**13** Rafting the Athabasca River

DAY 14
**14** Breakfast at Bear's Paw

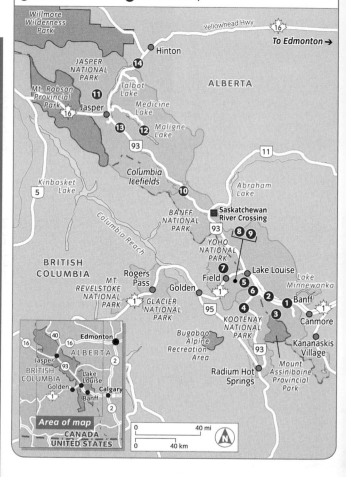

**L**ucky are those with time to linger in the Canadian Rockies. After all, there are nearly 23,000 sq. km (8,880 sq. ft.) of mountain wilderness to explore, and that takes time. Blending sightseeing with active adventures, and allowing you to roam from Banff up to Jasper, this is perhaps the ultimate 2-week vacation in this inimitable setting. Just be sure to book ahead of time, particularly your night at Yoho National Park's Lake O'Hara—either the campground or the historic and peerless Lake O'Hara Lodge. For more details see p 137.

**Day 1**
See Day 1 from the "Banff in 3 Days" tour, p 13.

**Day 2**
Aim to hit the trail today on horseback. See Day 2 of "Best in 1 Week," p 19.

**Day 3**
★★ kids **Sunshine Meadows.** When the snow melts at the world-famous Sunshine Village ski area, the alpine meadows blossom into a multicolored dreamland hugging the Continental Divide, great for hiking amidst more than 340 species of wildflowers. The Garden Path Trail is breathtaking in late July and August. To the south you can see Mount Assiniboine, the "Matterhorn of the Rockies." Take a bus from the parking lot or right from the Town of Banff. *Tip:* Book the morning buses ahead of time, and don't forget to bring a lunch, drink water, and use plenty of sunscreen. *8km (5 miles) west of Banff on the Sunshine Rd.* ☎ *403/762-7889. $25 adults, $15 children 3–12. June 19–Sept 15 daily 9am–5:30pm.*

*A family hiking in the Sunshine Meadows toward the vast, mountainous horizon.*

### Day 4

Less visited, and wonderfully expansive, Kootenay National Park is an off-the-beaten-path destination that makes a great day trip from Banff. This park is particularly friendly to families, with lots of kids in strollers and some great picnic spots.

### Travel Tip

Driving Hwy. 93 at dusk is prime wildlife-viewing time, so keep an eye out and drive safely.

Drive the Trans-Canada Hwy. 1 west to Castle Junction and take Hwy. 93 south. Length: 132km (82 miles) each way.

**1** ★ **kids** **Fireweed Trail.** A 20-minute loop explains why natural forest fires are healthy and good for the environment. As you continue on through Kootenay, you may be driving through a number of fire sites, so getting the low-down here will help you understand and appreciate the burned landscapes. ⏱ *15 min. 95km (59 miles) from Radium, on the Alberta–BC (and Banff–Kootenay) border.*

Continue southwest of Hwy. 93.

**2** ★★ **Stanley Glacier.** One of my favorite shorter hikes in the Rockies, this trail takes you from fire (a lightning-provoked burn from 1968) to ice (the Stanley Glacier) in just 2.5km (1.5 miles). Most of the 395 meters (1,296 ft) to be climbed are at the beginning, leaving you time to amble amidst a hanging valley with awesome views. Great for families. ⏱ *3 hr. Trail head is 3.2km (2 miles) west of the Alberta–British Columbia (and Banff–Kootenay national parks) border on south side of highway.*

**3** **Marble Canyon.** A narrow trail of limestone carved by two retreating glaciers, this is a great spot on a hot day. It's cool and shady. Kids will find this short hike intriguing, but keep an eye on them because the trail can get slippery. ⏱ *30 min. 89km (55 miles) from Radium, 7km (4⅓ miles) from Alberta–British Columbia (and Banff–Kootenay national parks) border on north side of highway.*

**4** ★ **Paint Pots.** Natives came together at these remote cold springs to gather ocher, an iron-based mineral that was baked, crushed, mixed with grease, and used as a paint for teepees, pictographs, and personal adornment.

*Natives once used the colorful minerals from these cold springs to make paints.*

*The soothing mineral waters of the Radium Hot Springs Pool.*

There's an excellent wheelchair and stroller-friendly 30-minute interpretive trail. 🕐 *40 min. 85km (53 miles) from Radium, 10km (6¼ miles) from Alberta–British Columbia (and Banff–Kootenay national parks) border on north side of highway.*

**⑤ ★★ Radium Hot Springs Pool.** Nestled in a canyon rich with oxide, these "sacred mountain waters" are surrounded by an orange-sunset vibe. The pools are more spacious than those in Banff, and there are often bighorn sheep mulling about. 🕐 *2 hr. See p 115.*

**⑥ Sinclair Canyon.** With this stunning farewell, Kootenay closes with a bang just shy of the village of Radium Hot Springs. Your car barely sneaks through iron-rich cliffs that are part of the Redwall Fault, and form a dramatic entrance to the Columbia Valley. There's a small roadside pull-off just west of the canyon where you can get out of the car to walk through the giant walls and take photos, which will be especially gorgeous at sunset.

Watch for bighorn sheep on the roadside. 🕐 *10 min. 1.5km (1 mile) from Radium and 131km (81 miles) from Alberta–British Columbia (and Banff–Kootenay national parks) border in the middle of the highway.*

**Day 5**
Travel from Banff to Lake Louise, following Day 3 of "Banff in 1 Week," p 16.

**Day 6**
**Hiking Paradise Valley/Larch Valley.** Rewarding and challenging, this hike starts in Paradise Valley, just south of Lake Louise. You'll take in a long list of highlights, like "Giant Steps," "Giant's Staircase," Lake Annette, and Horseshoe Meadows. It's a 17km (11-mile) hike that will take you all day. *See p 146. Trail head: Moraine Lake Rd 2.5km (1½ miles) south from Lake Louise Rd.*

**Day 7**
Visit Yoho National Park as described in Day 6 of "Best in 1 Week," p 19.

*Sinclair Canyon marks the striking exit out of Kootenay.*

*Paradise Valley's rolling waters and invigorating hiking terrain.*

## Day 8
**Camping at Lake O'Hara.** Just the mention of Yoho National Park's Lake O'Hara makes die-hard hikers get misty in the eyes. It's a great first-camping outing, since you access the backcountry campground via a Parks Canada–run bus—meaning you don't have to carry a heavy load and you can camp in comfort. The bus departs daily from a parking lot just off the Trans-Canada Highway at 8:30am, 10:30am, 3:30pm, and 5:30pm, and you must have a reservation. Once you've set up your tent and settled in, hike around the namesake lake for orientation, then head over past Schäffer Lake to beautiful Lake McArthur, a great 2- to 3-hour hike. *See p 108.*

## Day 9
**Hiking at Lake O'Hara.** Few places in the world can rival the stunning scenery, historic trail system, varied landscape, and special charm of this tiny area tucked beneath the Continental Divide. Spend your day on the Lake O'Hara Alpine Circuit, one of the best hikes in the entire world. It'll lead you past such glorious sites as the Opabin Plateau, the Yukness Ledges, and Lake Oesa. After taking the bus from just outside the Relais Day Shelter back to the parking lot (the last bus of the day leaves at 6:30pm), head back to Lake Louise. *See p 108.*

## Day 10
Today follows Day 3 of "Banff In 3 Days" (see p 16), but continues past the Icefields Centre and on to the Town of Jasper. Follow Hwy. 93, the Icefield Parkway, north 105km (65 miles) to Jasper townsite. You should have time to squeeze in the outstanding hike to Wilcox Pass as well, for a jaw-dropping lookout of the Columbia Icefields. See p 148.

## Day 11
Located in an expansive valley on the west bank of the Athabasca River, Jasper Townsite is quite large, but most visitors will stick to the two main drags, Connaught Drive and Patricia Street. That's where you'll find the good restaurants, shops, and outfitters.

❶ ★ **Jasper National Park Information Centre.** Stop here to pick up permits, maps, brochures and to have the friendly staff help you make the most of your day. ⏱ *20 min.* *500 Connaught Dr.* ☎ *780/852-6176.*

Head west across Connaught Drive (also known as Hwy. 93), continuing through the lights at the junction with Hwy. 16. Take the first right on Whistlers Road, continuing uphill until you reach:

**2 ★ Jasper Tramway.** Your quickest and easiest way to the high alpine terrain, this 7-minute gondola ride takes you up 973m (3,192 ft.), just short of the summit of the Whistlers Mountain. From the top, the views of the Athabasca and Miette valleys are stunning. There's a well-marked, though quite steep, 45-minute self-guided trail to the summit of the mountain. Watch for hoary marmots and white-tailed ptarmigan. Lineups can be intense, so try to head there in the morning. ⏱ *90 min. 3km (1¾ miles) south of Jasper on Hwy. 93, turn left/west on the Whistler Mountain Rd. for another 4km (2½ miles). ☎ 866/850-8726 and 780/852-3093. Adults $28, kids 5–14 $21. April 25–May 15 and Aug 30–Oct 12 daily 10am–5pm; May 16–June 25 daily 9:30am–6:30pm; June 26–Aug 29 daily 9am–8pm.*

Return to Hwy. 93 and head south 21km (13 miles) to the junction with Hwy. 93A, which heads north. Just past the turnoff is:

**3 Athabasca Falls.** Known more for its force than its height, this is one of the most impressive waterfalls in the Rockies, where the Athabasca River (the same one born at the Columbia Icefields and the most important river in Jasper National Park) thunders over a layer of hard quartzite and through a narrow limestone gorge. ⏱ *20 min. 25km (15 miles) south of Jasper.*

Continue north on the scenic Hwy. 93A 18km (11 miles) to the Cavell Rd., a narrow and winding mountain road that requires much attention from drivers. At 15km (9⅓ miles), you'll arrive at the parking lot beneath:

**4 ★★ Mount Edith Cavell.** This is the highest, and arguably the most scenic mountain in all of Jasper, named for a World War I British nurse. The Angel Glacier saddles the northeastern slope and sends a

*Mapping out a route at Jasper National Park's Information Centre.*

tongue of ice off the cliffside into a milky blue lake. The Path of the Glacier Trail takes you over boulders, shrubbery, pebbles, and sand through a landscape that, less than a century ago, was covered by a glacier. ⏲ *45 min. Follow Hwy. 93A to the Cavell Rd. Continue another 12km (7½ miles) to the parking lot.*

Take the Cavell Road back to Hwy. 93A. Turn left and continue 5.2km (3¼ miles) to the junction with Hwy. 93. Turn left and drive north into the Town of Jasper. Park your car next to the Heritage Railway Station. Cross Connaught Drive and walk up Miette Avenue to Patricia Street.

**5** ★ **Coco's Café.** Where laidback locals come to grab lunch, this busy little joint on Patricia St. has yummy wraps, curries, and soups that make superb lunches. There's also great cappuccino, latte, and espresso. The cafe is small and can be cramped; expect to literally rub elbows with your neighbors. *608 Patricia St.* ☎ *780/852-4550. $*

*Mount Edith Cavell, Jasper's tallest mountain.*

**6** ★ **Patricia Street.** Now that you've seen the major highlights south and west of town, spend the afternoon strolling the charming shops of Jasper's main streets. Focus on Patricia Street between Hazel Avenue and Cedar Street, then loop back along Connaught Drive. Slow down, enjoy the expansive views, and pick up a souvenir or two. **Counter Clockwise Emporium** (616 Patricia St.; ☎ 780/852-3152) has everything from books and jewelry to soaps and furniture.

Walking back towards your car, cross Connaught Drive at Miette Avenue and pop into the:

**7** **Heritage Railway Station.** Now housing the park administration offices as well as a train station, you can still picture Victorian ladies with their parasols and elaborate dresses mixing with rough 'n' tumble gold diggers at this old frontier outpost. Trains heading east and west across Canada, including the VIA Rail passenger trains, stop here daily. It's still a hub. ⏲ *10 min. On Connaught Dr. across from Whistler's Hotel.*

**8** **Old Fort Point.** Jutting out into the Athabasca River, the point offers great views that take in Jasper Townsite, Lac Beauvert, and the Fairmont Jasper Park Lodge. From here you can also catch sight of Mounts Kerkeslin and Hardisty to the southeast, and the snowy triangle of Mount Edith Cavell, shining above all others, to the south. It's a 2-hour hike atop a glacier-carved knoll to complete the loop via the lookout. Hike counter-clockwise for a gentler climb. ⏲ *2 hr. To access Old Fort Point, drive 5 minutes south of Jasper Townsite via Hwy. 93A and Old Fort Point Rd. See p 105.*

*Jasper's Heritage Railway Station transports visitors back in time.*

### Day 12

Take Connaught Drive east out of town until it joins with Hwy. 16, the Yellowhead Highway. Continue 4km (2½ miles) east to the bridge over the Athabasca River. Turn right. This is the beginning of the Maligne Valley Road.

**❶ ★★ Maligne Canyon.** A waterfall in slow motion, this limestone canyon is at the lip of the Maligne Valley as it meets the much lower Athabasca Valley. There is a lovely series of bridges and walkways that bring you close up to the largest underground drainage system known in Canada. At some points it's only 2m (6.5 ft.) across and 50m (164 ft.) deep! Starting at the upper bridge allows you to see the main highlights. Keep right at all intersections of the self-guided interpretive trail, and then loop back up. ⏱ *30 min. At km 7 (mile 4⅓) on Maligne Valley Rd.*

Continue south on the Maligne Valley Road until you reach:

**❷ Medicine Lake.** This could be called Mystery Lake—with no visible drainage, this lake seems to evaporate into nothing. The early Natives believed this mysterious lake had healing powers, hence the name. ⏱ *10 min. At km 21 (mile 13) on the Maligne Valley Rd.*

Continue south on the Maligne Valley Road until you reach:

**❸ kids ★★ Maligne Lake Cruise Spirit Island.** A 90-minute cruise on a glass-bottomed boat to a tiny, precious island, dotted with a handful of skinny pines and tucked in a placid corner of this glorious lake (the largest lake in Jasper National Park and the second largest glacial lake in the world), is a great outing for families. The island itself is shrouded in mystery and legends, which the guides explain en route. From the deck, watch for eagles, mountain goats, and even the odd avalanche, if it's the right time of year. ⏱ *90 min. At km 45 (mile 28) on the Maligne Valley Rd. Adults $55, kids 5–14 $27. Daily departures hourly from boat docks: thaw date—June 4 10am–3pm; June 5–June 30 and Sept 1–Oct 4 10am–4pm; July 1–Aug 31 10am–5pm.*

Return north on the Maligne Valley Road. Just before the Athabasca River bridge, turn left on Old Lodge Road. You'll pass lakes Annette and Edith before arriving at:

**❹ ★★ Jasper Park Lodge.** The largest commercial property in the Canadian Rocky Mountain National Parks, this classic wilderness lodge attracts tourists and dignitaries from around the world. Hike the hour-long walk around Lac Beauvert, rent a canoe for a paddle on the lake, enjoy a meal at one of the hotel's six restaurants, or play a round on the award-winning golf course. ⏱ *60 min. 3.2km (2 miles) west of Maligne Valley Rd on Old Lodge Rd.* ☎ *780/852-3301.*

**5** **Tea at the "JPL"** More cozy and casual than its sister hotels (the Banff Springs and the Chateau Lake Louise), tea here is likewise comfortable and delectable, with elegant sandwiches and pastries to accompany more than a dozen teas. Served daily between 2 and 4:30pm in the Emerald Lounge, overlooking Lac Beauvert, Mount Edith Cavell, and the Whistler's Mountain. *Old Lodge Rd.* ☎ *780/852-3301. $$*

### Day 13
**kids Rafting on Athabasca River** Take a scenic family float trip down the Athabasca River, or get the adrenaline pumping with the Class III rapids on the Sunwapta River. (Sunwapta is a Stoney Indian word meaning "turbulent river"). The big rapid is known as "the Whopper." *Jasper Raft Tours departs for the river daily at 12:30pm from the Jasper Railway Station. $55 adults, $20 youth 15–17, $15 kids 5–14, and $5 kids 4 and under. 604 Connaught Dr.* ☎ *780/852-2665; www.jasperrafttours.com.*

If rafting's not up your alley, book a round at the Fairmont Jasper Park Lodge's 18-hole course. *(4km/ 2½ miles east of Jasper Townsite on Hwy. 16, then south on Maligne Lake Rd. and a quick left/west after the bridge, follow 3.2km/2 miles to end; tee times daily 7am–6pm;* ☎ *780/ 852-6090; www.fairmont.com/jasper; green fees $110–$225).*

### Day 14
Grab breakfast at Bear's Paw (see p 127), 610 Connaught Dr; the original is still at 4 Cedar Ave.; ☎ 780/852-3233). If you are heading back to Banff, drive south along the Icefields Parkway, retracing your steps. It's 287km (178 miles) or 3.5 hours if you don't stop, but you'll likely discover the drive equally intriguing and beautiful in a southerly direction. Plan to stop for some photographing and leg-stretching. If you are heading to Edmonton, which is 370km (230 miles) and about 4 hours east, plan to stop for a soak at the Miette Hot Springs en route. See p 102. ●

*Testing out the award-winning golf course at Jasper Park Lodge.*

# 3 The Best
# Special-Interest Tours

# Banff **for Photographers**

Campground

Gasoline

Hospital/First Aid

(i) Information

▲ Mountain

Edmonton
ALBERTA
Jasper
BRITISH
COLUMBIA
Golden
Lake
Louise
Calgary
Banff
Area of
map
CANADA
UNITED STATES

Siffleur
Wilderness

**BANFF
NATIONAL
PARK**

Red Deer River

WAPTA
ICEFIELD

Bow River

Kicking
Horse
Pass

Field (i)

YOHO
NATIONAL
PARK

Lake Louise
Village

TEMPLE MTN.

KOOTENAY
NATIONAL
PARK

Castle
Junction

CASTLE
MTN.

CASCADE
MTN.

Lake
Minnewanka

Bow River

Kootenay Parkway

Vermillion River

Banff

MT. RUNDLE

**BANFF
NATIONAL
PARK**

ALBERTA
BRITISH
COLUMBIA

Mt. Assiniboine
Provincial Park

Marvel
Lake

MT.
ASSINIBOINE

Kootenay River

**DAY 1**

1 **Lake Minnewanka**
2 **Vermillion Lakes**
3 **Mt. Norquay Road**
4 **Surprise Corner**
5 **Eddie's Burger Bar**
6 **Cascade Gardens**
7 **Castle Mountain**
8 **Kootenay Parkway**

**DAY 2**

9 **Lake Louise**
10 **Moraine Lake**
11 **Trailhead Café**
12 **Herbert Lake**
13 **Peyto Lake**

*Previous page: Elk wander onto the Banff Springs Golf Course every spring.*

**B**anff National Park is one of the most photographed places in the entire world. Even amateur shutterbugs will be in delight here, where each turn brings another postcard-worthy view. Focusing in on the ultimate photo ops involves timing, patience, and flexibility. But if you get up early, and follow these stops, you'll surely gather a series of award-winners. START: **Town of Banff.**

## Day 1

**Head out of Banff on Banff Avenue, going northeast towards Cascade Mountain. Cross under the Trans-Canada Hwy. 1 and continue on:**

❶ **Minnewanka Road.** The easiest place for morning wildlife sightings is this drive just northeast of Banff. Watch for bighorn sheep near Two Jack Lake. A photo of Lake Minnewanka in a storm can be extremely dramatic.

**Continue across the Trans-Canada Highway to the second Banff exit. Turn right (west) on Vermillion Lakes Road and continue to where the road ends.**

❷ **Mount Rundle from Vermillion Lakes.** The stillness of the morning on these shallow lakes brings birdlife and moose. Late afternoon often offers alpine glow on the ridges of Rundle, that unforgettable peak that may be the most famous in all of Banff. In the summer you can paddle into the middle of the lake for an undisturbed shot—or skate out on the frozen lakes in the winter for an icy masterpiece.

**Take a left at Mount Norquay Road.**

❸ **Mount Norquay Road.** For a great shot that takes in all of the Town of Banff, as well as its scenic surroundings, head up the switchbacks of the Norquay Road to the turnoff.

**Drive back into Banff along Mount Norquay Road, which turns into Gopher Street and then becomes Lynx Street. Turn left at Buffalo Street and continue past Banff Avenue. After the housing ends, the forest thickens. At the next main switchback, park and get out of the car.**

❹ **Surprise Corner.** At an elbow bend on the edge of Tunnel Mountain, this is the classic viewpoint for admiring the Fairmont Banff Springs Hotel in all its glory. Sulphur Mountain forms the backdrop, and the majestic Bow Falls rumble beneath. Head up toward the Banff Centre on Buffalo Street, and keep an eye out for fellow photographers crossing the street!

*The afternoon glow of Mount Rundle's peaks can be captured from Vermillion Lakes.*

*Cascade Gardens at Canada Place with Cascade Mountain on the horizon.*

**Head back into town on Buffalo Street and turn left at Banff Avenue.**

🍵 **Lunch at Eddie's Burger and Bar** You're hungry and on a tight schedule. For a quick, hearty lunch, you can't beat the homemade burgers at this new joint in Banff. (See p 71.) 137C Banff Ave. (on *Caribou St.*). ☎ *403/762-2230.* *$$*

**Fallow Banff Avenue over the Bow River Bridge. Take a left at the end of the bridge and a quick right into the parking lot.**

**6** **Cascade Gardens.** At the far end of Banff Avenue, the landscaped gardens of Canada Place provide a great perspective on the hustle and bustle, not to mention the stunning background, of Banff's main drag. Cascade Mountain rises like a pyramid in the distance. Walk from the parking lot to a lookout across the Bow River Bridge. The gardens are open all day June through September and are free to visit.

**Drive back out of town, take the Mount Norquay Road, and then turn left (west) at the Trans-Canada Hwy. 1. The views begin from about 10km (6¼ miles) west of Banff.**

**7** **Castle Mountain.** There are many wonderful angles for capturing the many fine details of this beast of a mountain, between Banff and Lake Louise. With the Bow River in your foreground, there'll be many colors. Catch the late afternoon light from the west side of the Vermillion Pass, towards the British Columbia border from Castle Junction.

**Turn west on Hwy. 93 towards Radium Hot Springs.**

**8** **The Kootenay Parkway.** Hwy. 93 runs from Castle Junction to Radium Hot Springs in British Columbia, through Kootenay National Park. This is prime wildlife-viewing territory, particularly at dusk. White-tailed deer, bear, moose, coyotes, bighorn sheep, and mountain goats can all be seen. Key spots are at Moose Meadows picnic area, the inkspots near Hector Gorge, and the stretch between Crooks Meadows and Kootenay Crossing.

**Day 2**
**From the Town of Banff, head west on the Trans-Canada Hwy. 1 58km (36 miles) to Lake Louise. Turn off the highway and head up Lake Louise Road to the famous lake.**

**9** **Lake Louise** There's no wonder it's the most photographed lake in Canada. Beautifully framed by tall peaks, with a shimmering surface and a glacier at the back, come here mid-morning for the best light. Summer shots ought to include the boat dock at dawn. In winter, that means between 9am and noon. In summer, aim for a 7:30am start.

**Head down 2.5km (1½ miles) on Lake Louise Road, turning right on the Moraine Lake Road and following it for 13km (8 miles).**

**10** **Moraine Lake.** I've seen the image of this pristine lake on everything from the former $10 bill to a

# Photographing Wildlife

Depending on the time of year and your luck, you'll see a wide range of wildlife while roaming Banff National Park with your camera. June is ideal for black bears, and late fall is good for bull elks and moose. It's important, though, to respect park rules and always maintain a safe viewing distance from the animals. Usually, this means at least 30m (98 ft.), but for big animals like moose and bear, keep at least 100m (328 ft.) away.

beer advertisement. The Valley of the Ten Peaks in the background oozes with drama. Come before noon.

**Retrace your route and turn right on Lake Louise Road, returning to Lake Louise village.**

**11** **Trailhead Café.** Pick up lunch to go at this busy little cafe in Samson Mall. Grab a fresh wrap—there are more than a dozen to choose from, but I love the tropical wrap with chicken and mango salsa, or the donair wraps with lamb. They pack up nice and clean for a picnic later on. In Samson Mall. ☎ *403/522-2006*. *$*

**Head west on the Trans-Canada Highway and then north on the Icefields Parkway towards Jasper** to 2.5km (1½ miles) north of the Icefield Parkway gate.

**12** **Herbert Lake.** Because this lake is both small and sheltered by the tall peaks around it, it provides glass-like reflection in the morning, with the sun shining on the Bow Range in front, as well as Mount Bosworth to the north or Mount Temple and the peaks of Lake Louise to the south.

**Continue north on the Icefields Parkway another 39km (24 miles).**

**13** **Peyto Lake.** With a blue deeper than the waters of the Caribbean, and steep edges of mountain all around, Peyto Lake is a must-stop on the Icefields Parkway. In July and August, wildflowers are blooming. It's well worth the short stroll to the lookout.

*Photographers head to Lake Louise in the morning to capture a breathtaking view.*

# Banff **with Kids**

**DAY 1**

1 Sulphur Mountain Gondola
2 Banff Park Museum
3 Sushi Train
4 Biking on the Sundance Trail or Golf Course Loop
5 Fairmont Banff Springs Hotel
6 Grizzly House
7 Evening Interpretive Theatre

**DAY 2**

8 Hiking to Boom Lake

**DAY 3**

9 Lake Louise Sightseeing Gondola
10 Bill Peyto's Café
11 Columbia Glacier Icefield Experience

**F**amilies flock to Banff for adventure, nature, and quality time surrounded by inspiring fresh air. Lifelong mountain lovers are born here every day—just ask the locals, most of whom first fell for these peaks on a family vacation. The keys to keeping kids engaged include getting out of the car a lot, following your nose with a sense of adventure and discovery, and keeping track of all that you see and learn. START: **Your hotel in Banff.**

### Day 1

Drive south on Banff Avenue, over the Bow River Bridge. Turn left and then right quickly on to Mountain Road. Follow until it ends at:

**❶ Sulphur Mountain Gondola.** This may be your child's first summit, and the thrill won't soon be forgotten. After the 7-minute gondola ride drops you on top of the world, hike the 700 steps, across a secure boardwalk, to the top of Samson's Peak. ⏲ 90 min. See p 13.

Head back down Mountain Avenue, turning left onto Spray Road and right over the Bow River Bridge. Take a quick left onto Buffalo Street, then turn left into the parking lots between Central Park and:

**❷ Banff Park Museum National Historic Site.** Kids will

*Thousands of wildlife species are on display at the Banff Park Museum.*

like the discovery room inside this natural history museum, which is inside a log building built in 1903. With more than 5,000 species of birds, insects, and wildlife on display, it's a one-stop shop for learning about the Rockies. Great on a rainy day. ⏲ 45 min. See p 52.

You can leave your car parked next to the museum. Walk up Banff Avenue, turning right at Caribou Street. Half a block later, on your left-hand side is:

**❸ Sushi Train!** Family-friendly restaurants are a dime-a-dozen in Banff. But kids will love to choose pieces of sushi off a model train carrying the food around the counter at the tiny Sushi House Restaurant. Each dish is priced according to the color of the plate—and just ask the sushi master inside the tracks if there's something special you'd like. The food is fresh and healthy, and the atmosphere is convivial and fun. *304 Caribou St.* ☎ *403/762-4353. $.*

Walk to the west end of Caribou Street, turning left on Bear Street to the shop for:

**❹ Biking.** Kids love to try new things. Rent a bike in Banff and head up the Sundance Trail towards Sundance Canyon. The 3.7km (2.3-mile) trail has little elevation gain and is paved the entire way. Another option good for families is the 15km (9⅓-mile) Golf Course Loop. It's peaceful and pretty. *Adventures*

*At Sushi Train, diners select dishes that are delivered via a model railroad.*

*Unlimited (211 Bear St.; ☎ 403/762-4554) rents kids' bikes, trailers, and strollers.*

**After dropping off your bikes, return to your car. Drive back over the Bow River Bridge, taking a left onto Spray Road. Follow it until it ends at:**

**⑤ The "Castle in the Rockies."** Little girls will love to put on a party dress and explore inside the utterly distinctive Fairmont Banff Spring Hotel. Before you settle in for an English-style tea, roam medieval

*Enjoying a family-friendly bike route.*

corridors and find your way down mysterious corners. ⏱ *90min. Tea in the Rundle Lounge $32 for adults, $16 for children 6–12. 405 Spray Ave.* ☎ *403/762-6860.*

**From Banff Avenue, turn east or right on Wolf Street, then northeast or left on Tunnel Mountain Road. Drive 4km (2½ miles) to the entrance to Tunnel Mountain Campground:**

**⑥ Grizzly House.** Mixing Gilligan's island with Heidi's alpine shack, there is loads of personality here. It's noisy and raucous, great for energetic families. The specialties are cheese or beef fondues, but the most exotic version has you hot-dipping shark, alligator, rattlesnake, ostrich, and frogs legs. *207 Banff Ave.* ☎ *403/762-4055. $$.*

**⑦ Evening Interpretive Theater.** Nature interpreters from Banff National Park offer a variety of evening activities at the Tunnel Mountain Theatre, inside the Tunnel Mountain Campground. Throughout the summer, there are daily programs at 7:30pm, ranging from a historical rendition of Banff's legendary characters to stories of adventure in the peaks. They're fun, participatory, and a great learning experience. Best of all, they're free! ⏱ *45 min. Contact Parks Canada for updated schedules at ☎ 403/762-1550.*

## Day 2

**Grab a picnic lunch, some water, sunscreen, and your rain gear, and hit the trails. Drive west from Banff on the Trans-Canada Hwy. 1 28km (17 miles) to Castle Junction. Turn west onto Hwy. 93A S.**

### ❽ Hiking to Boom Lake.

Scores of life-long hikers have had their first thrills on the trail here in Banff. There are many kid-friendly hikes to choose from. I suggest the relatively gentle climb to Boom Lake, which is surrounded by a massive limestone wall along the Continental Divide. The trail has a real sense of discovery to it. Bring a picnic—it's a 10km (6.2-mile) return trip that will take you 4 hours or so. *Trail head is off Hwy. 93 S., 7km (4 miles) west of Castle Junction.*

## Day 3

**Head out of Banff, west on the Trans-Canada Hwy. 1 58km (36 miles) to the turnoff for Lake Louise. Turn right, heading up the hill to:**

### ❾ Lake Louise Sightseeing Gondola.

Kids are both scared and intrigued by grizzly bears, and this is a superb place to learn more about the often-misunderstood beast that rules the Banff backcountry. Interpretive guides explain how the "grizz" makes its home. ⏱ *2 hr. See p 63.*

**Drive down the hill, over the Trans-Canada Hwy. 1. At the main intersection, turn right on Village Road right past Samson Mall. Past the red-roofed Post Hotel, take a left into the entrance for:**

*This "snocoach" takes adventurous tourists into the Icefields.*

**❿ Bill Peyto's Café.** Located inside the Lake Louise Hostel and Alpine Centre, the food here is healthy, creative, and very reasonably priced for most budgets. The timber-framed room with stone fireplace makes for a relaxed, friendly atmosphere. Service is fast. Try the bison burgers, the chicken pesto burger, or the macaroni and cheese. There's also a kids' menu. *In the Lake Louise Hostel and Alpine Centre. 203 Village Rd.* ☎ *403/522-2200.* $.

**Exit Lake Louise, turning west or left onto the Trans-Canada Hwy. 1. Turn north on Hwy. 93, the Icefields Parkway, continuing for 130km (81 miles) until you reach:**

**⓫ The Columbia Glacier Icefield Experience.** Hop on a giant tractor called a "snocoach" with sky-high wheels, drive onto a frozen tongue of ice, and then hike out on the ice with crampons on — not your average day in the park. Tours leave every 15 minutes or so. It's best to visit the Icefield in the mornings or late afternoon to avoid the throngs of tourists arriving by bus from the towns of Banff and Jasper. *Tour lasts ⏱ 90 min. See p 17.*

# Banff **in Wintertime**

Campground
Gasoline
Hospital/First Aid
Information
Mountain
Point of Interest

Siffleur
Wilderness

93

WAPTA
ICEFIELD

Kicking
Horse
Pass

Field

Lake Louise
Village

BANFF
NATIONAL
PARK

YOHO
NATIONAL
PARK

TEMPLE MTN.

Castle
Junction

CASTLE
MTN.

Johnston
Canyon

CASCADE
MTN.

Ghost
River
Wilderness

Lake
Minnewanka

Banff

Park
Gate

1A

MT. RUNDLE

Canmore

Kootenay Parkway

93

KOOTENAY
NATIONAL
PARK

ALBERTA
BRITISH
COLUMBIA

Mt. Assiniboine
Provincial Park

MT.
ASSINIBOINE

Spray River

Marvel
Lake

Kootenay River

Park
Gate

Radium
Hot Springs

Edmonton

16        40
          16
Jasper              2
BRITISH        Lake
COLUMBIA       Louise
   Golden    1  Banff  Calgary
                        2
   1
        Area of
        map
CANADA
UNITED STATES

0                    10 mi
0                    10 km

**DAY 1**
**1** Mt Norquay
**2** Sleigh ride

**DAY 2**
**3** Ice skating
**4** Cross-country skiing
**5** Waldhause

**DAY 3**
**6** Ski Lake Louise

**DAY 4**
**7** Puppy Power
**8** Spa Power
**9** NHL Hockey

**DAY 5**
**10** Sunshine Village

**B**anff becomes a winter wonderland from late November through early April. Famous for its crisp blue skies, winter in the Canadian Rockies is just as beautiful as summer. In fact, many people swear that winter is an even better time to visit. For those not hindered by the cold, skiing in Banff is a one-of-a-kind experience. And don't forget all those snowmen and women waiting to be built and evening strolls waiting to be taken under star-studded skies, often active with the stunning *aurora borealis* ("northern lights").

## Day 1
**❶ Alpine Skiing at Mount Norquay.** A week is just barely enough to sample the best the area has to offer. Together, the three ski resorts in Banff — Mount Norquay, Sunshine Village, and Ski Louise — make this one of the great ski destinations in North America. I recommend visiting them each for at least a day. For Day 6, you could return to whichever you liked best (and that's an endless debate that rages on in Banff and will give you plenty to chat to folks about on the chairlift!). The SkiBig 3 partnership sells package to all three (☎ 877/754-7080 or 403/762-4561; www.skibig3.com). **Mount Norquay** is a locals' favorite because it's intimate and less than 15 minutes from Banff Avenue. Runs are steep. Economical ski-by-the-hour deals are good for days when you want to take

it easy. ☎ *403/762-4421. www.banff norquay.com. See p 157.*

## Evening 1
**❷ Sleigh Ride.** For a romantic winter evening, snuggle up under a cozy blanket with someone special, join a cowboy, and head out for a one-horse open-sleigh ride with Holiday on Horseback. *132 Banff Ave.* ☎ *403/762-4551. $27 adults, $23 children 4–12.*

## Day 2
**❸ Ice-Skating.** There are a number of places where you can skate outdoors under the winter sky. It's an exhilarating activity that's popular with families. Try the Vermillion Lakes, just outside the Town of Banff, in the early winter before the snow starts to pile up. Take

*Skating on Vermillion Lake.*

*Cross-country skiing just before sunset.*

Mount Norquay Road out of town, turning left on Vermillion Lakes Drive just before the Trans-Canada Hwy. 1. You can rent skates in Banff at **Snowtips** (225 Bear St.; ☎ 403/762-8177; from $14/day). At the Fairmont Chateau Lake Louise, there is an outdoor rink on the lake with a spectacular ice castle built right on top. It's a very scenic and romantic place to skate. *At the top of Lake Louise Dr. Rent skates at Chateau Mountain Sports inside the hotel.* ☎ 403/522-3837; from $9 for 2 hours or $12/day.*

❹ **Cross-Country Skiing.** A wonderful way to explore the park in winter, cross-country (or "Nordic") skiing promises great exercise, views—and solitude, if you're seeking it. There are more than 80km (50 miles) of managed trails in Banff National Park, many of them within a half-hour drive of Banff Townsite. The cross-country ski season runs from December to March. Try the Spray River Loop, which departs from the parking lot at Bow Falls, and the Shoreline Trail at Lake Louise, which starts just in front of the

Chateau Lake Louise. *See p 158 for ski-rental information.*

❺ On a crisp winter night, your cheeks aglow from a day in the mountains, what could be more divine than a steaming pot of Alpine-inspired fondue? The best fondue in Banff is at the **Waldhaus,** a Bavarian-style cottage in the woods beneath the Fairmont Banff Springs Hotel. *405 Spray Ave.* ☎ *403/762-6860. $$$. See p 70.*

### Day 3
❻ **Ski Lake Louise.** For jaw-dropping views, coupled with an incredibly varied terrain, head to this legendary ski resort across the valley from the infamous lake. Be sure to drop by cozy Temple Lodge for lunch. ☎ *800/258-7669 or 403/522-3555. www.skilouise.com. See p 157.*

### Day 4
❼ **Puppy Power.** It's one of the oldest forms of transportation in the

*Dog sledding outside of the Town of Banff.*

world. Dog-sledding is offered just outside Banff in Kananaskis Country. Drive the dogs or just ride along as you mush your way across a frozen lake. *Book through Snowy Owl Tours. ☎ 403/678-4369. www.snowyowl tours.com. 104-602 Bow Valley Trail, Canmore. $137–$220 per person.*

**❽ Spa Power** Work off all those kinks with a visit to the truly outstanding, private, and decadent **Willowstream Spa** at the Fairmont Banff Hot Springs. After soaking in the mineral pools, indulge in a mountain stone massage or an après-ski massage. *405 Spray Ave. ☎ 800/404-1772 or 403/762-2211. From $169 for 60 min.*

### Evening 3 or 4
**❾ NHL Hockey.** Hockey is a fast-paced game, and you'll catch some of the world's best ice hockey players in action at the Calgary Saddledome, cheering on the NHL's Calgary Flames. Pure Canadiana! *Book through Banff Adventures Unlimited (☎ 403/762-4554; www. banffadventures.com), which has shuttles from Banff for all Flames home games.*

Skiing through fresh powder at Sunshine Village.

### Day 5
**❿ Sunshine Village.** Tucked along the Continental Divide, beautiful Sunshine Village generally has the best snow, lots of good intermediate runs, and the notoriously extreme Delirium Dive, for experts only. Sunshine also has the best terrain park in the area and magnificent views of Mount Assiniboine. *☎ 800/661-1676 or 403/762-6500. www.skibanff.com. See p 158.*

## You Are in Avalanche Country

The Canadian Rockies is avalanche country. An extremely powerful wave of snow and ice that cracks off a mountain slope, an avalanche can destroy everything in its path. It's extremely challenging to predict when an avalanche might occur, and even more challenging to escape if you are caught in one. Drivers should avoid stopping in areas where Parks Canada has posted an AVALANCHE ZONE sign. Parks Canada updates avalanche forecasts regularly throughout the winter. In Banff, call ☎ 403/762-1460.

# Glaciers & Wildlife

To Jasper National Park

| | |
|---|---|
| 0 | 10 mi |
| 0 | 10 km |

Edmonton

ALBERTA

Jasper

BRITISH COLUMBIA

Golden

Lake Louise

Calgary

Banff

Area of map

CANADA

UNITED STATES

**Gasoline**

**Hospital/First Aid**

**Information**

**Mountain**

**Point of Interest**

**Skiing**

LYELL ICEFIELD

FRESHFIELD ICEFIELD

Saskatchewan River

Park Gate

Saskatchewan Crossing

Icefields Parkway

Siffleur Wilderness

Red Deer River

WAPTA ICEFIELD

YOHO NATIONAL PARK

Field

Kicking Horse Pass

Bow River

BANFF NATIONAL PARK

Lake Louise Ski Area

Lake Louise Village

TEMPLE MTN.

KOOTENAY NATIONAL PARK

Castle Junction

CASTLE MTN.

Johnston Canyon

Mount Norquay

CASCADE MTN.

Sunshine Village

Banff

Park Gate

**GLACIERS**

1. Mt. Temple
2. Mt. Victoria
3. Bath Glacier
4. Crowfoot Glacier
5. Bow Glacier
6. Snowbird Glacier
7. Saskatchewan Glacier
8. Columbia Icefield
9. Athabasca Glacier
10. Snow Dome

**WILDLIFE**

11. Urban Elk in Town of Banff
12. Minnwanka Loop
13. Muleshoe
14. Bourgeau Wildlife Overpass
15. Helen Lake
16. Bow Summit
17. Waterfowl Lakes
18. Mt. Coleman

**S**tudying the cycles of nature in the incredible mountain **wilderness** of the Canadian Rockies is enlightening, astounding, and inspiring. There are more than 1,000 glaciers in Banff, and all of them are retreating. Scientists say the glaciers of Banff lost 25% of their mass during the 20th century. Most can't be seen from the convenience of the major highways. There is, however, an easy-to-access selection with an interesting variety, ranging from hard-to-spot glaciers like the Snowbird to the most famous glacier in North America, the Athabasca. START: **Lake Louise.**

### Travel Tip

Most of these glaciers are northeast facing, so the light will be better for seeing them in the first half of the day.

**Glaciers in Banff National Park:**

**1 Mount Temple.** This may be my favorite peak in Banff. With a giant pyramid-like shape and a beautiful glacier below its summit, Mount Temple dominates the horizon south of Lake Louise. *6km (3¾ miles) east of Lake Louise on Trans-Canada Hwy. 1.*

**2 Mount Victoria.** One of the most photographed mountains in the world, this wide peak provides the scenic backdrop to Lake Louise. Always snow covered, it's best appreciated from the 5.3km (3.3-mile) hike to the Plain of the Six Glaciers, where the Aberdeen, Upper Lefroy, Lower Lefroy, Upper Victoria, Lower Victoria, and Pope's glaciers (as seen left to right or southeast to southwest) are all visible. It's a 4-hour round-trip that departs on the shore of Lake Louise just past the Fairmont Chateau Lake Louise, heading to the right around the lake. *See p 145.*

**3 Bath Glacier.** Part of the mighty Waputik Icefield, the Bath Glacier hugs the mid-ridge of Mount Daly. It can be seen at Mount Hector, just north of Lake Louise. *17km (11 miles) north of Lake Louise on Hwy. 93.*

**4 Crowfoot Glacier.** Years ago, there were three toe-like extensions of this glacier clinging to the side of a cliff. The lowest "toe" has retreated completely, leaving a rare two-toed crow. *32km (20 miles) north of Lake Louise on Hwy. 93.*

**5 Bow Glacier.** Visible at the back of the valley behind Num-Ti-Jah Lodge, the Bow Glacier is the same glacier that originally carved out the entire Bow Valley (which you've

*Upper Bow Lake with the Bow Glacier in the background.*

*Hiking on Parker Ridge with the Saskatchewan Glacier in the background.*

driven through as you came north-west from Banff) 10,000 years ago. For a closer view, hike the 4.6km (2.9-mile) trail to Bow Glacier Falls, which starts just behind Num-Ti-Jah Lodge. *36km (22 miles) north of Lake Louise on Hwy. 93.*

⑥ **Snowbird Glacier.** Clinging to the east face of Mount Patterson, just north of Bow Pass, the beautiful Snowbird Glacier drapes over a cliff, with wings that are limited in size by the width of each ledge. Only the left wing is visible from the highway, best seen 3.1km (2 miles) north of the Silverhorn Creek Bridge, on the west side of the highway at the bottom of the hill past Bow Summit. *48km (30 miles) north of Lake Louise on Hwy. 93.*

*Tourists climb the Columbia Icefield.*

⑦ **Saskatchewan Glacier.** The longest tongue of ice flowing off the Columbia Icefields, this is a classic outlet valley glacier. The best view is from Parkers Ridge, a superb 2.7km (1.7-mile) hike from the highway. *117km (73 miles) north of Lake Louise on Hwy. 93. See p 147.*

⑧ **Columbia Icefield.** The largest frozen ice mass south of the Arctic Circle, this icefield measures 325 sq. km (125 sq. miles). It includes six glaciers: Athabasca, Saskatchewan, Dome, Columbia, Castleguard, and Stutfield. *125km (78 miles) north of Lake Louise on Hwy. 93. See p 99 for more information on experiencing the Icefields.*

⑨ **Athabasca Glacier.** The most famous glacier in North America is in Jasper National Park. It's also the easiest glacier to access—more than 10,000 people visit this frozen river of ice each busy summer day. *125km (78 miles) north of Lake Louise on Hwy. 93. See p 99.*

⑩ **Snow Dome.** Also in Jasper National Park, this peak is a hydro-logical apex. One of only two in the world, water flows in three directions: north to the Arctic Ocean, east to the Atlantic Ocean, and west to the Pacific Ocean. The Dome Glacier can be seen on Snow Dome's north side as you approach the Columbia Icefields from the north on Hwy. 93.

**B**anff is no zoo! Here, animals roam free, and the natural rhythms of the wilderness are maintained. There are 53 species of wild mammals in Banff, 13 of which are on Parks Canada's "Species at Risk" list. Count yourself lucky if you catch any wildlife sightings in Banff. But if you follow this list, your chances will be higher. Dawn and dusk are the best times of day for spotting wildlife. Be sure to keep track, and report all wildlife sightings to Parks Canada at ☎ 403/762-1470. START: **Town of Banff.**

### Wildlife in Banff National Park:

**⑪ Urban Elk in Town of Banff.** During certain times of the year (mainly spring and summer), elk make their way into the heart of the Town of Banff. The drive around the Banff Springs Golf Course is a prime area for spotting these magnificent mammals. *At the end of Golf Course Dr. past Bow Falls.*

**⑫ Minnewanka Loop.** Just northeast of the Town of Banff, the drive along the Minnewanka Road is particularly good for seeing bighorn sheep who often gather near Two Jack Lake, 12km (7½ miles) from Town of Banff on Minnewanka Loop. *Take Banff Ave to the northeast out of town. It turns into Minnewanka Loop after going under the Trans-Canada Hwy.*

**⑬ Muleshoe.** An open pasture off the Bow Valley Parkway Hwy. 1A,

this is a good spot for coyotes, elk, and mule deer. Birders also come here to spot Western Tanagers and Hammond's flycatchers. *Take the Trans-Canada Hwy. 1 5.5km (3½ miles) west of Banff to the Bow Valley Pkwy. Hwy. 1A. Continue for 5.5km (3½ miles) to Muleshoe Picnic Area.*

**⑭ Bourgeau Wildlife Overpass.** This is one of two specially-designed tree-covered bridges that go over the Trans-Canada Hwy. 1 west of Banff and allow wildlife like bears, elk, coyotes, wolves, cougars, and moose to roam freely in their natural habitat. They're aimed to reduce the large number of mammals (and humans) that were being killed by vehicles, and they've been extremely successful. While you can't stop to take a look at the bridge, do drive slowly and keep your eyes open. There are also 22

*Bull elk feeding in Central Park.*

*A male bighorn sheep in Banff National Park.*

underpasses between Banff and Lake Louise. *11km (6¾ miles) northwest of Banff on the Trans-Canada Hwy. 1.*

⓯ **Helen Lake.** From the high alpine environment of this hiking trail near the Crowfoot Glacier, you'll be tramping through prime grizzly bear habitat, and may also spot white-tailed ptarmigan, grouse, and golden eagles. *33km (21 miles) north of Lake Louise on the Icefields Pkwy. See p 147.*

⓰ **Bow Summit.** Following the short interpretive trail to the Peyto Lake and on to the Bow Summit lookout, you may be able to see cute little mammals like pikas (which look like miniature rabbits) and hoary marmots. *41km (25 miles) north of Lake Louise on the Icefields Pkwy.*

⓱ **Waterfowl Lakes.** You won't be surprised to see mallard ducks and loons on these lakes. What may well surprise you, however, is spotting a moose. Summer evenings are the best time. *58km (36 miles) north of Lake Louise on the Icefields Pkwy.*

⓲ **Mount Coleman.** From the picnic area at its base, mountain goats can be spotted clinging precariously to the cliff of this peak. *100km (62 miles) north of Lake Louise on the Icefields Pkwy.* ●

# Bear Jams: Keep Moving, People!

**Everybody's thrilled to catch a glimpse of a bear in the wild.** In the Canadian Rockies, there are more "bear jams" than "traffic jams" as tourists pile up in their vehicles to snap photos of grizzlies or black bears, creating chaos on the roads. Whistling, yelling, running about . . . tourists behave strangely in the presence of a magnificent mammal, causing problems that can turn fatal for the bear and for other drivers. If you see a bear and want a closer look, slow down safely but do not stop. Give the bear space. The moment one car stops, everybody stops. No matter the circumstances, stay in your vehicle and do not approach the bear. Once alerted to the sighting of a bear, Parks Canada staff and often the police will appear at the scene and urge travelers to keep moving. Remember to call in a bear sighting to ☎ 403/762-1470.

# The Town of Banff

| | | |
|---|---|---|
| **1** Banff Information Centre | **7** Old Banff homes | **13** Canada Ski Museum West |
| **2** Bow River Promenade | **8** Nestors Market | **14** Banff Avenue |
| **3** Central Park | **9** Whyte Museum | **15** Three Ravens Wine Bar |
| **4** Banff Park Museum | **10** Canada Place Gallery | **16** Banff Centre for the Arts |
| **5** Cascade Gardens | **11** Old Crag Canyon | |
| **6** Bow Falls | **12** Cascade Plaza | |

*Previous page: Cyclists stop to enjoy the view of Moraine Lake.*

**T**he Town of Banff is the beating heart of Canada's first and most important national park. Planned and organized as a resort town from the beginning, the focus here remains on pleasing visitors. There are historic and natural highlights dotted around the outskirts of town, but the center of all things is bustling Banff Avenue, the main drag. Here, tourists speaking dozens of language nip in and out of shops, pop into a pub for a pint, get their skis and bikes tuned up and enjoy some truly fabulous cuisine. START: **Park your car in the parking lot behind the information center.**

**❶ ★★ Banff Information Centre.** This is a must for your first stop of the day. In the heritage building in the heart of "downtown" Banff, it's a great orientation center, with helpful desks staffed by the friendly folks at Parks Canada and the Banff-Lake Louise Tourism Bureau. They have maps, brochures, and trail updates, and they can help you decide what to do when. At the back, there's a short video that will also help you get your bearings and understand just why this place is so important. 🕐 *20 min.* **224 Banff Ave.** ☎ *403/762-1550. Daily in winter 9am–5pm; spring and fall 9am–7pm; summer 8am–8pm.*

Exit the Information Centre and cross Banff Avenue at the lights at corner of Wolf Street. Continue down Wolf St. 3 blocks, crossing

Bear and Lynx streets, until you reach:

**❷ Bow River Promenade.** The canoe docks mark the beginning of a gentle, paved trail that follows one of Canada's most important rivers. The beautiful Bow River is the longest river in Banff National Park. From its headwaters at Bow Lake, 90km (56 miles) north of the Town of Banff, it flows south and east, passing through Banff, Canmore, and Calgary. It joins the South Saskatchewan River and eventually drains into the Atlantic Ocean, on Canada's east coast. This promenade makes for a good stroll.

Follow the trail downriver, around the bend to:

**❸ Central Park.** Site of Canada Day parties, weddings, picnics, and

*A couple enjoys a walk along the Bow River.*

*Canada Place's Cascade Gardens.*

Frisbee-tossing, this is Banff's main outdoor meeting space. During the summer, there are often outdoor concerts here, and Parks Canada's "Roving Interpreters" often set up shop at one of the picnic tables (you'll spot them in their red and green uniforms). Sometimes there are elk feeding here, too! ⏲ *15 min. Along the north shore of the Bow River btw. Banff Ave. and Bow Ave. parallel to Buffalo St.*

*One of Banff's original heritage homes.*

Next to the park, on the east side between the park and Banff Avenue, is:

**④ kids ★★ Banff Park Museum.** A beautiful building dating to 1903 and reflecting early Rocky Mountain architecture, this is the oldest natural history museum in Western Canada. It houses an incredibly complete collection of wildlife. It's also a superb rainy-day option. Come for a good look at beaver's teeth or an elk's antler. ⏲ *30 min. 91 Banff Ave.* ☎ *403/762-1558. Oct 1–May 15 daily 1–5pm; May 15–Sept 30 daily 10am–6pm. Adults $3.90, seniors $3.40, youth $1.90. Free for children under 6.*

**Cross over the Bow River Bridge. Cross Mountain Road and head through the iron gate for a visit to:**

**⑤ Cascade Gardens.** Inspired by the geological history of the Rockies, this lovely garden includes a series of fountains, or "cascades" that are an essential part of appreciating the architecture and design of the Banff Administration Building. During summer, the local Siksika First Nation erects a traditional tee-pee here with an interesting cultural exhibit. ⏲ *30 min. At the T-intersection where Spray and Cave aves.*

*Some of the cheeses available at Nestor's Market.*

meet Banff Ave, just over the Bow River Bridge. Daily 24 hours. Free admission.

**Back across Mountain Road, turn right (east) before crossing the bridge, following the trail 1.2km (.8 miles) to:**

**6** ★ **Bow Falls.** Tucked in behind the Fairmont Banff Springs Hotel, **Bow Falls** will let you escape the hustle and bustle of the busy Banff Townsite. The 10m (33-ft.) falls, eroding between two rock formations, roar and wash away any tension you may have picked up. The rock on the left bank of the river is 245 million years old, while the one on the right bank is some 320 million years old. Beneath the falls, the Fairmont Banff Springs Golf Course dominates the southern side of the valley.

**Walk back up river. At the Bow River Bridge, take the east (or downriver) sidewalk, and begin exploring the historic neighborhoods of "old Banff," along Beaver and Muskrat streets.**

**7** **Old Banff homes.** Along Buffalo Street, backing onto the Bow River, are some of the most spectacular homes in Western Canada. Remember, Banff has a "need to

reside" rule — only people with jobs in Banff can live here. At 313 Buffalo St. is a home dating to 1920 that was once the Park Superintendent's Residence. At the corner of Buffalo and Muskrat streets, you'll find the historic Grant-Hemming home, built in 1921 from local materials (note the Rundlestone steps and river-stone chimney). Next door are legendary naturalist and climatologist Norman Sanson's Home and the summer residence of Senator Amedée Forget.

**8** If you were drawn to one of the riverside picnic tables along the Bow River, drop into **Nestor's Market**. With a deli, bakery, and plenty of fresh produce, you can put together a superb lunch to go. *122 Bear St.* ☎ *403/762-3663. Daily 8am–11pm. $*

**Walk back to the Bow River trail at the end of Muskrat Street, and continue along the river, passing Central Park. On Lynx Street, turn right to:**

**9** ★★ **Whyte Museum of the Canadian Rockies.** This museum houses excellent exhibits about the human history of Banff and has a

*Old Crag Cabin, built in the 19th century.*

tremendously wealthy archive of memoirs, sketches, photographs, and personal artifacts of Rocky Mountain pioneers, visionaries, and artists. Changing exhibits shine light on how the mountains have inspired generations. Another excellent rainy-day activity. ⏲ *90 min. 111 Bear St.* ☎ *403/762-2291. Daily 10am-5pm.Admission $7 adults, $4 seniors and students, free for children 6 and under.*

**Cross Lynx Street and head down the lovely Bear Street. On the left-hand side, a few shops down, you'll find:**

**⑩ ★ Canada Place Gallery.** Even if you aren't a dedicated art collector, it's worth taking time to explore this fine arts shop and gallery. Featuring exclusively Canadian art, the focus is on landscape, contemporary, and Native styles. It's not hard to understand how the Rockies inspire these artists. There are often opening receptions for the public on Saturday afternoons. ⏲ *20 min. 201 Bear St.* ☎ *403/762-3757. Mon–Thurs 9:30am–6pm; Fri and Sat 9:30am–7pm; Sun 11am–6pm. www.canadahouse.com.*

**⑪ Old Crag Cabin.** Built between 1888 and 1890, this tiny wooden cabin is one of the most storied buildings in Banff. Home to the weekly newspaper from 1901 to 1929, it was restored and relocated in 1999 and is now the "downtown" home and box office for the Banff Centre. ⏲ *5 min. 211 Bear St.* ☎ *403/762-6301. Tues–Sun 11am–6pm.*

**Follow Bear Street to its terminus at Wolf Street and head into:**

**⑫ Cascade Plaza.** For a quick and affordable pick-me-up, jump into the food court at the basement of Banff's biggest mall. You'll find a dozen different counters serving everything from sushi and pizza to curries. You can buy lunch for under $5! *317 Banff Ave.* ☎ *403/762-8484. $.*

*The entrance to Banff's Whyte Museum.*

Before riding the escalators up, start at the bottom floor display for:

**⑬ Canadian Ski Museum West.** From early wooden telemark skis to the latest World Cup victories, the history of Banff's favorite sport is told in displays throughout the three-story Cascade Mall. Start at the first floor and work your way up to follow in chronological order. You may even bump into a real ski legend or two while roaming about Banff. ⏲ 20 min. 317 Banff Ave. ☎ 403/762-8484. Mon–Thurs 10am–7pm; Fri and Sat 10am–9pm; Sun 11am–7pm. Free admission.

Exit the mall and turn right to stroll:

**⑭ Banff Avenue.** Home to great shops, cafes, restaurants, historic buildings, and a general hustle-and-bustle, take time to stroll the scene and eavesdrop on dozens of languages on one of Canada's iconic main drags. A massive redevelopment project in 2007 widened the sidewalks and made street life more pleasant.

Head up Wolf Street and turn right on St. Julien Road. Follow the curving road until you enter the campus of the Banff Centre.

**⑮ ★ Three Ravens Wine Bar** For a quick pre-concert bite to eat or a cocktail, or a post-event glass of wine and dessert, you can't beat this scenic restaurant above the Sally Borden Building in the Banff Centre. It wins for the best restaurant view in Banff, by far. Try a glass of pinot noir from the Okanagan with Spanish paprika beef rolls. *At the Banff Centre on St. Julien Rd.* ☎ 403/762-6300. Daily 4pm–midnight. $$.

*An opera performance at the Banff Centre.*

**⑯ Banff Centre for the Arts.** Part of the town's fabric for nearly a century, this is a world-renowned arts, culture, and educational institution that hosts celebrated musicians, writers, and other artists from around the world on a regular basis. The Centre's Summer Arts Festival showcases the best in a variety of artistic areas—from costume design and creative writing, to drama and opera, to jazz and classical music. It's another place where the mountains truly awaken inspiration and creativity. Don't miss the chance to take in a truly inspiring performance, often in the outdoors, during your visit to Banff. *St. Julien Rd.* ☎ 403/762-6100. *www.banffcentre.ca.*

# Lake Minnewanka

0    1 mi
0    1 km

••• *Walking Path*

BANFF
NATIONAL
PARK

▲ CASCADE
MOUNTAIN

*Lake Minnewanka Loop*

*Lake Minnewanka*

*Two Jack Lake*

Trans-Canada Highway

*Johnson Lake*

Banff Ave.

Tunnel Mountain Rd.

BANFF

1. Hoodoos
2. Bankhead
3. Lake Minnewanka
4. Stewart Canyon
5. Johnson Lake

**S**ome call it a giant bathtub, but Minnewanka does offer unique activities and a chance for open skies. It's the biggest lake in Banff National Park, created by nature and later expanded by humanity. The Minnewanka Loop makes a nice tour from the Town of Banff, and can be done in a leisurely 2 or 3 hours. To extend it, add in the hike to C-Level Cirque or another of the hikes listed in chapter 6. Watch for bighorn sheep on the road near Two Jack Lake—and remember not to feed them. **START: Town of Banff. Head east off Banff Avenue on Tunnel Mountain Road.**

**1 Hoodoos.** The mysterious pillars look like they've been dropped from outer space. In fact, they are freestanding posts made of silt, gravel, and rocks cemented together by dissolved limestone. The uncemented particles were slowly eroded and washed away. There is a paved, stroller-friendly 500m (1,640-ft.) trail to a nice viewpoint that also offers lovely views of Mount Rundle and the Bow River. *Just off Tunnel*

*Mountain Rd. past the entrance to Tunnel Mountain Campground Village I, 4km (2½ miles) east of Banff.*

**Tunnel Mountain Road continues to loop around until it meets up again with Lake Minnewanka Road, which passes under the Trans-Canada Highway (Hwy. 1) and goes northeast along the side of Cascade Mountain. Pull off Lake Minnewanka Road after 3km (1¾ miles).**

*Mount Rundle, the Bow River, and the Hoodoos from the Hoodoo Trail Overlook.*

**2 Bankhead.** Once the working center of Banff, Bankhead was a small settlement that boomed in the early 20th century. Old machinery and foundations are still in place, such as the entranceway to the former church and the transformer building, which features a display about coal mining. A short 10-minute walk about the area, following interpretive displays, will help bring the history to life.

**Continue down the road another 2.6km (1½ miles) and pull into the parking lot in front of:**

**3 Lake Minnewanka.** This lake used to be called "The Lake of the Water Spirits" by the Stoney Nation, who apparently feared these spirits and refused to swim in or boat on the lake. Early Europeans took a likewise timid view, calling it "Devil's Lake." Although it's too cold for a dip, boaters today have no fear. This is the only lake in Banff where motorboats are allowed. From May through October, you can take an enclosed boat trip to the end of the lake. ⏱ *90 min.* ☎ *403/762-3473. $44 for adults, $19 for children 6–15, free for children under 6.*

**To the north of the parking lot is a day use area with picnic tables and shelters. Continue through to reach the trail for Stewart Canyon.**

**4 ★ Stewart Canyon.** A nice 30-minute round-trip walk along the lakeshore takes you to this canyon, named for the first superintendant of Banff National Park. Much of the canyon has lain underwater since Minnewanka was dammed, first in 1895 and again in 1912 and 1941. The highlight is the giant wooden truss bridge. The trail is very accessible (even to wheelchairs).

**Returning to the parking lot, head across the causeway, past Two Jack Lake. At 2.4km (1½ miles) from Minnewanka, turn left to:**

**5 Johnson Lake.** Not to be confused with Johnston Canyon, which is farther west, this man-made lake is perhaps the best place for a swim on a hot day. A 3.5km (2.1-mile) trail circles the lake; walk counterclockwise to take in views of Cascade Mountain.

*An inukshuk at Lake Minnewanka.*

# Bow Valley Parkway

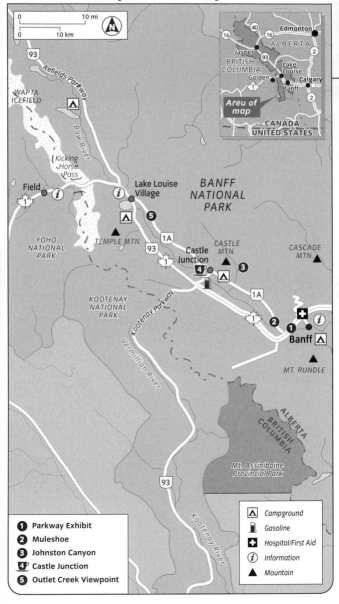

1 Parkway Exhibit
2 Muleshoe
3 Johnston Canyon
4 Castle Junction
5 Outlet Creek Viewpoint

Campground
Gasoline
Hospital/First Aid
Information
Mountain

The Bow Valley Parkway ("Hwy. 1A") is less congested than the Trans-Canada Hwy. 1, although the two roads run parallel along the Bow River. Built in 1920—the first road connecting Banff and Lake Louise—this 51km (32-mile) route still feels more like a mountain road than an expressway. The 13 interpretive stops along the way are each worthwhile. I've selected the best of the bunch. The drive will take about 3 hours, including stops. START: **Town of Banff.**

Head left (north) on Mount Norquay Road out of the townsite and turn left (west) onto the Trans-Canada Highway (Hwy. 1). You'll meet up with the Bow Valley Parkway about 5km (3 miles) from town.

**❶ Parkway Exhibit.** Westbound travelers can make a quick stop at this turnoff to orient themselves to the route ahead. There is a good map and a refresher on the etiquette of wildlife encounters. .9km (½ mile) from start of Bow Valley Pkwy.

**❷ ★ Muleshoe.** A short 1km (.6 mile) trail starts across the highway from the picnic area and explores the remnants of the 1993 prescribed fire. 5.5km (3½ miles) from start of Bow Valley Pkwy.

**❸ ★ Johnston Canyon.** A walkway leads up this canyon, past two large waterfalls carved through limestone bedrock. The first part of the trail is on a paved surface and is a very gentle climb that ends at the first waterfall, called the Lower Falls. There are interpretive signs on the way up to the Upper Falls, almost twice the height of the Lower Falls and a further 1.6km (1 mile). 18km (11 miles) west of Banff Townsite.

**❹ Castle Junction.** Three important roads meet here—the Bow Valley Parkway, Hwy. 93, and the Trans-Canada Hwy. 1. There's a gas station, a small convenience store, and cozy cabins. It's also a good

place to pick up picnic supplies. 28km (17 miles) from Town of Banff. ☎ 403/522-2783. $

**❺ Outlet Creek Viewpoint.** Here you'll find a grand view of towering Mount Temple, the third highest peak in Banff National Park. Known as Morant's Curve, the S-bend in the Canadian Pacific Railway tracks below here offers a classic photo when eastbound trains motor through the valley. 46km (29 miles) from the start of the Bow Valley Pkwy.

*The 98-foot high upper falls of Johnston Canyon.*

# Lake Louise

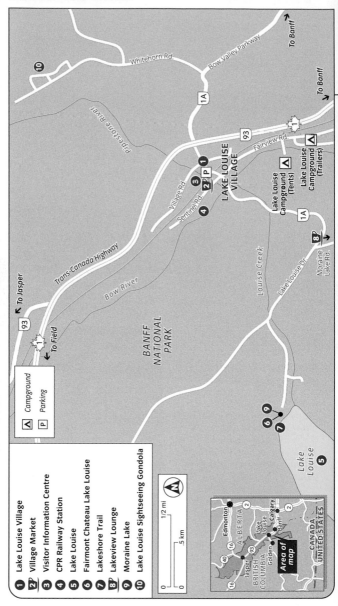

1. Lake Louise Village
2. Village Market
3. Visitor Information Centre
4. CPR Railway Station
5. Lake Louise
6. Fairmont Chateau Lake Louise
7. Lakeshore Trail
8. Lakeview Lounge
9. Lake Louise Sightseeing Gondola
10. Lake Louise Sightseeing Gondola

△ Campground
P Parking

**Y**ou can't come to Banff and not see placid, beautiful Lake Louise. Situated 56km (35 miles) northwest of the Town of Banff, Lake Louise is perhaps the most photographed lake in the country, one that people from all over the world associate with their image of Canada. It's also the name of the small village just below the lake. While many people drive out just to snap a photo and then return to their hotel, it deserves a full day, with at least a short hike and tea time. START: **Lake Louise Village parking lot.**

**1 Lake Louise Village.** Consisting of the key elements of a small village (or "hamlet," as Parks Canada refers to it), here you'll find gas stations, a grocery and liquor store, post office, some apartments, an ATM, restaurants, a book shop, and an outdoor equipment store. And let's not forget some outstanding hotels—which, admittedly, you might not expect to find in a small village or "hamlet." See p 78 for Lake Louise hotels.

**2 Village Market.** Amidst the trail maps and souvenirs, pop into this grocery store for picnic supplies. Although not as well stocked as the grocery stores in Banff, you can get some dips, veggies, simple sandwiches, snacks, and drinks to fill your backpack. ☎ 403/522-3894. 101 Lake Louise Dr. $.

**3 ★ Visitor Information Centre.** Housed behind Samson Mall, Parks Canada's main outpost in Lake Louise has a ton of information, including exhibits and a theater presenting the geological history of the Canadian Rockies. You can also pick up permits and maps, as well as trail, weather, and road reports. 101 Lake Louise Dr. ☎ 403/522-3833. Daily Sept 26–April 30 9am–4pm; May 1–June 18 and Sept 13–26 9am–5pm; June 19–Sept 6 9am–8pm; Sept 7–12 9am–7pm.

Follow Lake Louis Drive through the 4-way stop, pass beneath the railway overpass, and turn right

*Inside a Samson Mall shop in Lake Louise Village.*

immediately onto Sentinel Drive. Follow this road for 1.4km (¾ mile).

**4 CPR Railway Station.** The oldest building in Lake Louise is the log station across the tracks from the village core. Built in 1910, it was a working terminal for more than 60 years. A National Historic Site, the station is now home to a restaurant in summertime. (*No street no.*) Sentinel Rd. ☎ 403/522-2600.

It's about 8km (5 miles) or a 5-minute drive from the village up to the lake itself and the often-crowded parking lot.

**5 ★★★ Lake Louise.** In summer, thousands of people empty out of bus tours in front of the lake each day to have their picture taken, then jump back on to the bus and head off to the next tour stop. It's quite crowded. But the lake is so beautiful and pristine, you should go anyway. Fed by glacial meltwater, Lake Louise is 2.4km (1½ miles) long, 500m (1,640 ft.) wide, and 90m (295 ft.) deep. Behind it is **Mount Victoria**, at an elevation of 3,464m (11,365 ft.), with the thick **Victoria Glacier** on its front ridge. The lake was named after Princess Louise Caroline Alberta (1849–1939), the fourth daughter of Queen Victoria and later the wife of the governor-general of Canada.

**6 ★ Fairmont Chateau Lake Louise.** Often called a "diamond in the wilderness," this is an impressive and important hotel rich in history and obviously blessed with an incredible setting. If you aren't a guest, you are welcome to come in for a meal, some shopping or tea, or just to roam and wonder at the fantastic ambience.

**7 ★ Lakeshore Trail.** This is a 2km (1.2 mile) path (each way) and runs from the Chateau along the lake's north shore to the western end of the lake. At the back of the lake, quartzite crags are popular with rock climbers. It's open to walkers May through October, and to skiers the rest of the year.

**8** It's quite civilized inside the **Lakeview Lounge,** a superb place for an afternoon tea at the Chateau Lake Louise. The view, stretching across the lake, is divine. Traditional afternoon tea service includes sandwiches, scones, sweets, and polished silver. ☎ 403/522-1818. *Tea served daily 12–4pm. $$$.*

There is a winding road (open only May–Oct) that takes you the 13km (8 miles) from Lake Louise to Moraine Lake. At the often-crowded parking lot are a lodge,

*Inside the Victoria Ballroom at Chateau Lake Louise.*

*A hiker takes a break overlooking Moraine Lake.*

a picnic area, and some interpretive exhibits.

**9 ★★★ Moraine Lake.** Just south of Lake Louise is another stunning alpine lake, situated in front of the Valley of the Ten Peaks. Wild and dramatic, Moraine Lake is very popular. You can rent canoes here for $35/hour, or walk an excellent interpretive trail to the Moraine Lake Rockpile for the view that used to be on the Canadian $20 bill. Moraine Lake is also the trail head for a number of the best hikes in Banff National Park (see chapter 6).

Head back to the Lake Louise Road, down to the village, over the Trans-Canada Hwy. 1 and up Whitehorn Road to:

**10 ★★ kids Lake Louise Sightseeing Gondola.** Take a gondola to the summit of Whitehorn Mountain for excellent views of the Bow Valley, Lake Louise, and the Continental Divide. Naturalists lead guided hikes that are great interactive learning experiences. Grizzly bears have been known to hang out here in the summer, so going with a guide is a wise idea. *At the top of Whitehorn Rd.* ☎ *403/522-3555. www.lakelouisegondola.com. May 15–Sept 30 daily 9am–5pm. $25 adult, $13 child 6–15, free for kids under 6.*

## The History of the Chateau

The Chateau Lake Louise had humble beginnings, in the form of a cabin built on the site in 1890 by the CPR (Canadian Pacific Railway). By 1917 the cabin had burned to the ground, and a hotel with all the modern amenities of the day was erected in its place. While the Banff Springs Hotel, also run by the CPR, was to be luxurious, the CPR marketed the Chateau Lake Louise as a destination for outdoor adventurers. Mountaineers, artists, and horseback riders flooded in, giving the Chateau a level of popularity and character that the Springs is still striving for. With a feel akin to the Swiss Alps, mountain culture is alive and well here.

# The **Icefields Parkway**

**Campground**

**Gasoline**

**Hospital/First Aid**

*(i)* Information

**Mountain**

**Point of Interest**

1. Crowfoot Glacier
2. Bow Lake
3a. Bow Summit
3b. Peyto Lake
4. Waterfowl Lake
5. Mistaya Canyon
6. Saskatchewan Crossing
7. Weeping Wall
8. Big Bend and Big Hill
9a. Sunwapta Pass
9b. Jasper National Park border
10. Athabasca Glacier

**T**he landscape you see on the spectacular **Icefields Parkway** is the kind that used to dominate western North America. Hwy. 93, the Icefields Parkway, connects Banff and Jasper National Parks, and along the way you'll be wowed by raging rivers, turquoise lakes, glacier-clad summits, and massive icefields. The hiking trails and the wildlife viewing are outstanding. This tour only covers the highway as far as the Icefields Centre. For information on continuing on to Jasper, see p 98. START: **Lake Louise.**

### Travel Tip

If you haven't already got one, pick up a detailed map and guide to the Icefields Parkway from the Lake Louise Visitors Centre, in Lake Louise's Samson Mall (101 Lake Louise Dr.; ☎ 403/522-3833).

**Continuing north on the Icefields Parkway, the road steadily climbs higher and higher and the views become more and more dramatic as you make your way through three river valleys and pass beneath towering glacier-topped peaks.**

**❶ Crowfoot Glacier.** This is the first of a long lineup of glaciers you'll see. There are interpretive signs posted at the roadside viewpoint. It's a good spot to contemplate the shrinking of the world's glaciers and

the impact of climate change. *33km (21 miles) north of the Trans-Canada Hwy. 1 junction at Lake Louise.*

**❷ ★ Bow Lake.** This ice-blue lake is the third-largest in Banff National Park. Almost all of its water is glacier-fed; you can just see the Bow Glacier at the back of the lake. It's a nice place for a picnic. The red-roofed inn on the lake's northeast shore is Num-Ti-Jah Lodge (see p 81). *34km (21 miles) north of the Trans-Canada Hwy. 1 junction at Lake Louise.*

**❸ ★★ Bow Summit and Peyto Lake.** At an elevation of 2,069m (6,788 ft.), you're at the highest point in Canada that can be crossed by a highway year-round. Walk the short interpretive trail at Bow Summit to see this beautifully turquoise lake set far below the lookout in a deep glacial valley. It's named for pioneer guide "Wild" Bill Peyto, who

*Sunrise at Crowfoot Mountain and Crowfoot Glacier.*

*Bow Lake, the third-largest in Banff National Park.*

was a warden in Banff National Park. Continue further along a short extension of the trail, going left and up the hill, for views of the glacier that feeds the lake. *40km (25 miles) north of the Trans-Canada Hwy. 1 junction at Lake Louise.*

**Heading north past Peyto Lake, the landscape becomes more barren and beautiful.**

❹ **Waterfowl Lake.** Stop at the pullout next to this serene lake to view some of the mighty peaks along

*The Mistaya River descends through Mistaya Canyon.*

the Continental Divide. In fact, all of the mountains on the west side of the Icefields Parkway form part of the backbone of the continent. From here, you can see Howse Peak and Mount Chephren, a classically horned peak resembling a pyramid. *56km (35 miles) north of the Trans-Canada Hwy. 1 junction at Lake Louise.*

❺ ★ **Mistaya Canyon.** Deep and steep, the beauty of this canyon is in its sublimely curvy walls, the fierce roar of the water, and in the quiet trail, much quieter than at the other famous canyons in the Rockies. The Mistaya River drops off Bow Summit and has carved out a series of potholes along the canyon's walls. A steep but short .5km (.3 mile) trail leads from the north end of a parking lot on the west side of the Icefields Parkway down into to the canyon. *71km (44 miles) north of the Trans-Canada Hwy. 1 junction at Lake Louise.*

❻ **Saskatchewan Crossing.** On the banks of the Saskatchewan River, there is a warden station, gas station, snack bar, and gift shop at a roadside complex called "The Crossing." It's a good place to get out and stretch your legs. *77km (48 miles) north of the Trans-Canada Hwy. 1 junction with the start of the Icefields Pkwy. 93.*

**Pull over on the west side of the highway to get a look at:**

**7 Weeping Wall.** In summer you may see only a few drops of water wetting the ridge on the east side of the highway, but in the winter these drips and drops freeze to create a huge frozen waterfall draped in layer upon layer of ice. This is a hot spot for the technical sport of ice climbing. *106km (66 miles) north of the Trans-Canada Hwy. 1 junction at Lake Louise.*

**8 Big Bend and Big Hill.** A famous hairpin turn is followed by a steep hill, both of which are excruciatingly difficult for cyclists. There is a pullout at the top of the hill with a nice view of Bridal View Falls. *111km (69 miles) north of the Trans-Canada Hwy. 1 junction at Lake Louise.*

**9 Sunwapta Pass and Jasper National Park.** At 2,023m (6,637 ft.), this is the second highest point on the Icefields Parkway and forms the border between Banff and Jasper national parks. It's also the border between the two watersheds: The North Saskatchewan River drains from here to Lake Winnipeg, Hudson Bay, and the Atlantic Ocean, while on the other side of the pass the Sunwapta River eventually makes its way to the Arctic Ocean. It's all downhill from here—108km (67 miles) north on the Icefields Parkway 93 to Jasper

*Water streaming down The Weeping Wall.*

Townsite. *122km (76 miles) north of the Trans-Canada Hwy. 1 junction at Lake Louise.*

**10 ★★ Athabasca Glacier.** With its tongue almost touching the highway, this is the most accessible of the six principal glaciers that make up the Columbia Icefields, and is also the most visited glacier in North America. It's receding 2 to 3m (6½–9¾ ft.) each year. Park your car at the Toe-of-the-Glacier trail head (which was covered by ice in the 1950s) and walk down through lunar-like landscape to the ice. Don't venture onto the ice without a guide (see sidebar). *127km (79 miles) north of the Trans-Canada Hwy. 1 junction at Lake Louise.*

## Icewalk Interpretive Tours

More adventurous folk will prefer to join a certified mountain guide who leaves daily from the Toe-of-the-Glacier parking lot for guided hikes that allow you to walk on the ice. Three- to 4-hour hikes cost $60 for adults and $30 for kids 7 to 16 (kids under 7 not allowed). More strenuous—and more exploratory—6-hour hikes cost $70 for adults, $35 for kids 7 to 16. Call ☎ 800/565-7545 or see www.icewalks.com.

# Dining in **Banff National Park**

*Closed in Winter*

••• Walking Path

0      1/4 mi

0      .25 km

Grizzly House **18**
Juniper Bistro **2**
Le Beaujolais **24**
Maple Leaf Grill **20**
Melissa's **13**
Nourish **10**
Phil's **27**
Old Spaghetti House **8**
Post Hotel **3**
Saltlik **12**
Sleeping Buffalo **7**
Sukiyaki House **9**
Sundance Bistro **26**
Tom Wilson
  Steakhouse **4**

The Balkan **23**
Baker Creek Bistro **1**
Barpa Bills **14**
The Bison Mountain
  Bistro **15**
Bow Valley Grill **29**
Bumper's **5**
Cilantro's **6**
Coyotes Grill **19**

Cozy Cave Bake
  Shop **16**
Eddie's Burger and
  Bar **21**
Eden at Rimrock **28**
Elk & Oarsmen **22**
Evelyn's **11**
Fuze Finer Dining **25**
Giorgio's Trattoria **17**

# Dining Best Bets

Best **Bakery**
Cozy Cave Bake Shop $ 208 Bear St.
(p 71)

Best **Breakfast**
★★ Coyotes $$ 206 Caribou St.
(p 71)

Best **Brunch**
★★ Bow Valley Grill $$ In the Fairmont Banff Springs Hotel. 405 Spray Ave. (p 70)

Best **on a Budget**
Sundance Bistro $ 102 Spray Ave.
(p 75)

Best **Burger**
★ Eddie's Burger and Bar $ 137C Banff Ave. (p 71)

Best **Canadiana Cool**
★★ Maple Leaf Grill $$ 137 Banff Ave. (p 72)

Best **Charcuterie Plate**
★ Sleeping Buffalo $$$ 700 Tunnel Mountain Rd., at the Buffalo Mountain Lodge (p 74)

Best **for Health Freaks**
Nourish $$ 215 Banff Ave., 2nd floor (p 73)

Best **Italian**
★ Giorgio's $$ 219 Banff Ave. (p 72)

Best **for Locavores**
★★ The Bison Mountain Bistro $$$ 211 Bear St. (p 70)

Best **for Parents with No Babysitter**
Old Spaghetti House $ Cascade Plaza, 317 Banff Ave., 2nd floor (p 74)

Best **Patio**
Juniper Bistro $ In the Juniper Hotel, bottom of Mount Norquay Rd. (p 73)

Best **Pizza**
★ Cilantro's $$ 700 Tunnel Mountain Rd. at the Buffalo Mountain Lodge (p 71)

Best **Pub Food**
★ Elk & Oarsmen $$ Upstairs, 119 Banff Ave. (p 72)

Best **Salad Bar**
Bumper's $ 603 Banff Ave. (p 71)

Best **Splurge**
★★ Eden at Rimrock $$$ In the Rimrock Resort Hotel, Mountain Ave. (p 72)

Best **Steakhouse**
★ Tom Wilson Steakhouse $$$ At the Chateau Lake Louise, 111 Lake Louise Rd. (p 75)

Best **Sushi**
Sukiyaki House $$ In the Park Ave. Mal, 211 Banff Ave., 2nd floor (p 75)

Best **Takeout**
Barpa Bills $ 233 Bear St. (p 70)

Best **Wine Cellar**
★★★ Post Hotel $$$ 200 Pipestone (p 74)

*Seafood from Maple Leaf Grill.*

# Restaurants A to Z

**kids The Balkan** BANFF *GREEK*
The recipes at this family-owned
Banff landmark come from the old
country—souvlaki, moussaka, arni
psito, and donair pitas (great for
lunch). This is a great place for sharing. A new decor oozes Mediterranean sunshine. On Tuesdays and
most Thursdays, the place comes
alive with belly-dancing and plate-
smashing. *120 Banff Ave.* ☎ *403/
762-3454. Entrees $14–$29. AE, MC,
V. Daily 11am–11pm. Map p 68.*

**★★★ Baker Creek Bistro** LAKE
LOUISE *REGIONAL* Fresh and modern food is served by warm and
friendly folks inside a heritage cabin
just south of Lake Louise. It's definitely
worth the drive from Banff, and
makes a great pit-stop on your way to
Lake Louise or the Icefields Parkway.
*11km (6¾ miles) southeast of Lake
Louise and 14km (8¾ miles) north of
Castle Junction on the Bow Valley
Pkwy., Hwy. 1A.* ☎ *403/522-2182.
Entrees $16–$32. AE, MC, V. Daily
noon–3pm and 5–9pm. Map p 68.*

**Barpa Bills** BANFF *GREEK* For
something "to go," you can't beat a
souvlaki in a warm pita, hot off the
grill at this little Bear Street joint. It's
topped with fresh tzatziki sauce and
cooked to order. There are also
gyros, burgers, and poutine, a
French-Canadian specialty. Grab a
stool at the counter if you want to
eat in, but don't expect friendly
chatter with the staff! *233 Bear St.*
☎ *403/762-0377. Entrees $6–$14.
No credit cards. Daily 11am–9pm.
Map p 68.*

**★★ The Bison Mountain Bis-
tro** BANFF *REGIONAL* Regional
and seasonal "Rocky Mountain comfort food" is perfectly suited for
Banff. The classic dish is grilled
bison rib steak. Or try daily game.
Everything except the pickles and
mayonnaise is made from scratch.
The outdoor patio is the nicest in
town. Downstairs is a deli and sandwich shop. *211 Bear St.* ☎ *403/762-
5550. Entrees $16–$45. AE, MC, V.
Mon–Fri 11am–10:30pm; Sat–Sun
10am–10:30pm. Map p 68.*

**★★ Bow Valley Grill** BANFF
*CANADIAN* With an open concept
kitchen and a gorgeous setting

*The Bison Mountain Bistro, home to "Rocky Mountain comfort food."*

*A dish from the Fairmont Banff Springs' Bow Valley Grill.*

inside the Fairmont Banff Springs, this is the best brunch in town. Summertime brings market-style buffets. In wintertime, it's a la carte. *In the Fairmont Banff Springs Hotel, 405 Spray Ave. ☎ 403/762-6860. Entrees $24–$46. AE, DISC, DC, MC, V. Daily 6:30am–2pm, 6–9pm; Sunday brunch 11am–2pm. Map p 68.*

**kids** **Bumper's** BANFF *STEAK-HOUSE* If a place has been serving visitors Alberta beef at affordable prices since 1975, it's got to be on to something good. Simple meals star Alberta beef: Prime rib, a half-dozen cuts of steak, and baby back ribs are the usual go-to choices. They also have the best salad bar in town. *603 Banff Ave. ☎ 403/762-2622. Entrees $10–$40. AE, MC, V. Daily 5–10pm. Map p 68.*

★ **Cilantro's** BANFF *CALIFOR-NIAN* Next to the Buffalo Mountain Lodge, this is a cozy cafe perfect on a warm summer's evening. Pizzas from the apple-wood-fired oven are the best items on the menu, with deep crusts and creative ingredients. *At Buffalo Mountain Lodge, corner of Tunnel Mountain Dr. and Coyote Dr. ☎ 403/762-2400. Entrees $15–$19. AE, MC, V. April 1–June 7 Fri–Sun 5–10pm; July 4–Aug 31 Wed–Sun 5–10pm. Closed Sept 1–Dec 16. Map p 68.*

★★ **Coyotes Grill** BANFF *SOUTH-WESTERN* Fresh, healthy, relaxed, and very popular with locals, Santa Fe comes to the Rockies here with corn and chile peppers on enchiladas, in soups, and even on pizzas. There's also a superb breakfast. *206 Caribou St. ☎ 403/762-3963. Entrees $16–$28. AE, MC, V. Daily 7:30am–11pm. Map p 68.*

**Cozy Cave Bake Shop** BANFF *BAKERY* Pick up scrumptious treats from cupcakes to cinnamon rolls, as well as picnic-worthy sandwiches and tea-time loaves. *208 Bear St. ☎ 403/762-0414. Sandwiches $6–$12. MC, V. Daily 10am–6pm. Map p 68.*

★ **Eddie's Burger and Bar** BANFF *BURGERS* Build your own gourmet burgers well into the evening at this fun and funky bar. The bison burger comes with sautéed mushrooms, double-smoked bacon, and roasted garlic aioli on an English muffin. Add sweet potato fries and a milkshake. *137C Banff Ave. (on Caribou St.). ☎ 403/762-2230. Entrees $8–$16. MC, V. Daily 11:30am–3am. Map p 68.*

*The luxurious Eden at Rimrock.*

*Evelyn's is a favorite for coffee or lunch.*

**★★ Eden at Rimrock** BANFF
*FRENCH* Request table no. 2 at
Banff's most luxurious restaurant for
views and romance. The refined
French-influenced menu ranges
from three- to eight-course tastings
at Western Canada's only 5-diamond
CAA/AAA award winner. *Rimrock
Resort Hotel, 300 Mountain Ave.*
☎ *403/762-1840. Tasting menus
$100–$300. AE, DC, MC, V. Daily
6–10pm. Map p 68.*

**★ Elk & Oarsmen** BANFF *PUB*
Settle in with some locals to watch
the game and dig into the best pub
food in Banff. Recommended
choices are the Black Angus steaks
or a burger (you have elk, bison,
beef, salmon, or chorizo to choose
from!). There's a great patio on the
rooftop, regular happy-hour specials, and big screen TVs. *Upstairs,
119 Banff Ave.* ☎ *403/762-4616.
Entrees $10–$27. AE, MC, V. Daily
11am–11pm (pub stays open later).
Map p 68.*

**Evelyn's** BANFF *COFFEE-
SHOP* Where Banff locals head for
a coffee, Evelyn's now has three
locations around town. The two
Banff Avenue locations often have
long lineups of tourists looking for
caffeine. Quieter is the shop
beneath the movie theater, known

as Evelyn's Too. Lunch items include
thick fresh sandwiches and daily
soup specials. *229 Bear St.* ☎ *403/
762-0330. Entrees $8–$12. MC, V.
Daily 7am–6pm. Map p 68.*

**★ Fuze Finer Dining** BANFF
*FUSION* With a giant open-concept
space and an impressively international sensibility, expect surprises
here, like Thai risotto or an Indian-
spiced steak. Those with a sense of
adventure should opt for the tasting
menus and wine pairings. *110 Banff
Ave., 2nd floor.* ☎ *403/760-0853.
Entrees $26–$65. AE, MC, V. Daily
5:30–10pm. Map p 68.*

**★ Giorgio's Trattoria** BANFF
*ITALIAN* Since a new chef took
over, Giorgio's is more relaxed, fresh,
and simple. Dine Italian family-style
by sharing dishes like an antipasto
platter, risotto, and a wood-fired
pizza. Don't want to share? Then you
can't miss the Tuscan Caesar salad
and veal scaloppini. *219 Banff Ave.*
☎ *403/762-5114. Entrees $15–$40.
AE, MC, V. Daily 5–10pm. Map p 68.*

**Grizzly House** BANFF *FONDUE*
Fondue has never gone out of style
at this over-the-top alcove on Banff
Avenue. Veggie, chicken, prawn,
beef, even buffalo can get dropped
into the pot. There's plenty of

retro-shtick here to temper the steaming pots of fondue and the smoking hot plates. Things can get rowdy and noisy in here, though. *207 Banff Ave.* ☎ *403/762-4055. Entrees $15–$48. AE, MC, V. Daily 11:30am–midnight. Map p 68.*

**Juniper Bistro** BANFF *CANADIAN* Just out of town, the main draw to this bistro is its sunny patio, one of the nicest in town. The menu has hearty pub food, like dark ale bison ribs and a fish hot pot. *Bottom of Mount Norquay Rd. in the Juniper Hotel.* ☎ *403/763-6205. Entrees $23–$34. AE, MC, V. Daily 7:30am– 9:30pm. Map p 68.*

**Le Beaujolais** BANFF *FRENCH* Banff's long-standing fine dining establishment has fancy and good French food, but the atmosphere doesn't live up to the food or the prices. Better is the new bistro next door known as Café de Paris, with a more unpretentious version of their menu, better prices, and a great Alberta AAA entrecote special. *Corner of Buffalo and Banff sts.* ☎ *403/762-5365. Fixed 2-course menu $55, 3-course menu $65. AE, MC, V. Daily 5–10pm; Sat and Sun noon–4pm. Map p 68.*

★★ **Maple Leaf Grill** BANFF *CANADIAN* Canadian classics like rainbow trout and venison vie with Alberta bison and Atlantic salmon beneath a birchbark canoe in a room that feels more like a lodge. Although casual in atmosphere, the food is decidedly upscale. There's an award-winning wine list with over 100 Canadian labels. *137 Banff Ave.* ☎ *403/760-7680. Entrees $18–$48. AE, DISC, MC, V. Daily 10am–2am. Map p 68.*

★ **kids Melissa's** BANFF *STEAK-HOUSE* Since 1930, Melissa's has been specializing in steaks—you choose the cut and the sauce (peppercorn or mushroom, among others); it comes with fries and a salad. They also have a great breakfast menu and a kids' menu. *218 Lynx St.* ☎ *403/762-5511. Entrees $12–$26. DC, MC, V. Daily 7am–10pm. Map p 68.*

**Nourish** BANFF *VEGETARIAN* If you're tired of steaks and gamey meat, this friendly second-floor restaurant in the Sundance Mall has organic, vegan, wheat-free, and gluten-free choices. Even non-vegetarians will like the nacho platter or wild-mushroom ravioli with lavender

*The Caribou Room at Maple Leaf Grill.*

*Nourish has excellent vegetarian options.*

sauce. The decor is funky and colorful. *215 Banff Ave.* ☎ *403/760-3933. Entrees $12–$25. AE, MC, V. Wed–Mon noon–3pm and 5–9pm. Map p 68.*

★ kids **Phil's** BANFF *CANADIAN* Nothing is fancy at Phil's. Think spaghetti with meatballs, a chicken breast with gravy and mashed potatoes, or beef liver with bacon and onions. Breakfast portions are massive. With free baby food, crayons, lots of booster seats, and an excellent kids' menu, families can't find a better spot. *109 Spray Ave.* ☎ *403/762-2902. Entrees $9–$15. AE, MC, V. Daily 6:30am–8pm. Map p 68.*

kids **Old Spaghetti House** BANFF *ITALIAN* Expect no-frills Italian specialties like lasagna and pesto linguini. Entrees all include soup or salad, garlic bread, and an ice cream dessert. There are always great specials and bargains here, especially for families. *Cascade Plaza, 317 Banff Ave., 2nd floor.* ☎ *403/760-2779. Entrees $10–$16. AE, MC, V. Daily 11:30am–10pm. Map p 68.*

★★★ **Post Hotel** LAKE LOUISE *REGIONAL* Blending fine dining with a rustic elegance, the Swiss chef uses European techniques and regional ingredients, mainly meats like veal tenderloin, caribou striploin, and rack of lamb. Service is first-class. The real star, though, is a massive wine cellar. *200 Pipestone.* ☎ *403/522-2167. Entrees $37–$52. AE, MC, V. Daily 11:30am–2pm and 6–10pm. Map p 68.*

**Saltlik** BANFF *STEAKHOUSE* With a modern, trendy twist, steaks here are fast-cooked in a 1,200°F (649°C) infrared oven. Top it with a marinade like chipotle barbecue or citrus rosemary. A lounge downstairs features live jazz and martinis. *221 Bear St.* ☎ *403/762-2467. Entrees $21–$44. AE, MC, V. Daily noon–1am. Map p 68.*

★ **Sleeping Buffalo** BANFF *REGIONAL* One of the earliest promoters of Rocky Mountain cuisine, there is an impressive selection of very local meats here. The sample platter has smoked buffalo, venison ham, and elk salami. An incredibly tender bison rib-eye stands out in the entrees list. *700 Tunnel Mountain Rd. at the Buffalo Mountain Lodge.* ☎ *403/760-4484. Entrees $26–$40. Daily 7–11:30am, noon–10pm. Map p 68.*

**Sukiyaki House** BANFF *JAPA-NESE*  The best traditional Japanese food in Banff. The Love Boat—a wooden board filled with a wide variety of sushi, including sashimi and maki, plus vegetable tempura—easily feeds two hungry hikers and comes with miso soup and rice. *211 Banff Ave., 2nd floor, Park Ave. Mall.* ☎ *403/762-2002. Entrees $14–$34. AE, MC, V. Daily 4:30–10pm. Map p 68.*

**Sundance Bistro** BANFF *CANADIAN*  Great value just 100m (328 ft.) from Banff Avenue, this bistro is inside the Y Mountain Lodge and offers up sandwiches (hot and cold) as well as burgers and daily specials like meat pies and pastas. Portions are large. For breakfast try the huevos rancheros. *102 Spray Ave.* ☎ *403/762-3560. Entrees $12–$24. MC, V. Daily 7am–9pm. Map p 68.*

**★★ Tom Wilson Steakhouse** LAKE LOUISE *STEAKHOUSE*  A spacious new option at the Chateau Lake Louise is all about Alberta's famous beef, although the best cut is actually a bison tenderloin. A

*The patio at Sundance Bistro.*

starter selection of tapas is practically enough for a meal on its own. "The Feast" for two includes ribs, beef sirloin, bison, shrimp, and salmon. *111 Lake Louise Rd., in the Fairmont Chateau Lake Louise.* ☎ *403/522-1818. Entrees $21–$49. AE, DISC, DC, MC, V. Fri–Tues 6–9pm. Map p 68.*

*Tapas from the Tom Wilson Steakhouse.*

# Lodging in **Banff National Park**

Banff Alpine Centre 3
Baker Creek Chalets 22
A Banff Boutique Inn –
    Pension Tannenhof 12
Blue Mountain Lodge 11
Buffalo Mountain Lodge 5
Buffaloberry Bed & Breakfast 6
Driftwood 7
Fairmont Banff Springs Hotel 14
Fairmont Chateau Lake Louise 19

Fox Hotel and Suites 8
Hidden Ridge Resort 4
Johnston Canyon Campground 9
Lake Louise Alpine Centre 18
Lake Louise Campground 21
Num-Ti-Jah Lodge 15
Post Hotel 20
Rimrock Resort Hotel 13
Rundlestone Lodge 1
Skoki Lodge 17
Storm Mountain Lodge 23
Tunnel Mountain
    Village Campground 2
Two Jack Campground 10
Waterfowl Lake Campground 16

# **Lodging** Best Bets

Best **Backcountry**
★★ Skoki Lodge $$ *In Banff National Park; access from trail head at Temple Lodge next to Lake Louise Ski Resort (p 82)*

Best **Boutique Hotel**
★ A Banff Boutique Inn—Pension Tannenhof $$ *121 Cave Ave. (p 78)*

Best **on a Budget**
★ Blue Mountain Lodge $ *327 Caribou St. (p 79)*

Best **for Business**
Rimrock Resort Hotel $$$ *300 Mountain Ave. (p 81)*

Best **Historic Charm**
★★ Post Hotel $$$ *200 Pipestone (p 81)*

Best **for Families**
Fox Hotel and Suites $$ *46 Banff Ave. (p 80)*

Best **for Meeting Hiking Partners**
Banff Alpine Centre $ *801 Hidden Ridge Way (p 78)*

Best **Local Knowledge**
★ A Banff Boutique Inn—Pension Tannenhof $$ *121 Cave Ave. (p 78)*

Best **Night's Sleep**
Buffaloberry Bed and Breakfast $$ *417 Marten St. (p 79)*

Best **Scenery**
Num-Ti-Jah Lodge $$ *Icefields Pkwy. (p 81)*

Best **Spa**
★★ Willow Stream at the Fairmont Banff Springs $$$ *405 Spray Ave. (p 79)*

Best **View**
★★ Fairmont Chateau Lake Louise $$$ *111 Lake Louise Dr. (p 79)*

Best **for Wildlife Watching**
★ Baker Creek Chalets $$ *11km (6¾ miles) southeast of Lake Louise and 14km (8¾ miles) north of Castle Junction on the Bow Valley Pkwy., Hwy. 1A. (p 78)*

*The hot pool at Fox Hotel & Suites.*

# Lodging A to Z

## Banff Alpine Centre

BANFF   Fun and reasonably priced, this hostel is just outside the Banff Townsite on Tunnel Mountain Road. Dorm rooms sleep four to six people, and there are five double rooms with private baths that are a good bargain. The pub is always lively. *801 Hidden Ridge Way.* ☎ *403/762-4123. www.hihostels.ca/alberta. 52 units, which accommodate btw. 2 and 6 people, or 216 beds. Beds from $28 private doubles from $111. MC, V. Map p 76.*

## ★ kids Baker Creek Chalets

LAKE LOUISE   In a semi-secluded spot just south of Lake Louise, this collection of red-roofed cabins and lodges is really amidst the wild—bears, elk, and deer routinely stroll

by. Cabins mainly sleep four to six and have kitchenettes. It's the kind of place you want to settle in and spend an entire week, well worth at least a night or two away from busy Banff. The train runs sporadically throughout the day and night next to the property; if you are a light sleeper, ask for their quietest cabins. *11km (6[bf]3/4 miles) southeast of Lake Louise and 14km (8¾ miles) north of Castle Junction on the Bow Valley Pkwy., Hwy. 1A.* ☎ *403/522-2270. www.bakercreek.com. 35 units. Doubles $260–$335. AE, MC, V. Map p 76.*

## ★ A Banff Boutique Inn—Pension Tannenhof

BANFF   A local couple with a passion for inn-keeping has turned an old-fashioned building into a lovely inn, with modern decor and mountain hospitality. It's a breath of fresh air in Banff. Rooms have strange layouts, some with very small bathrooms, but the vibe is relaxing and breakfasts superb. *121 Cave Ave.* ☎ *403/762-4636. www.banffboutiqueinn.com. 10 units. Doubles $185–$310. Breakfast included. MC, V. Map p 76.*

*Inside a cabin at Baker Creek Chalets.*

★ **Blue Mountain Lodge** BANFF
Offering simple, clean, and pleasant
rooms, the owners at this little place
go the extra mile, from a superb
breakfast to afternoon home-baked
snacks and free wireless. Just steps
from Banff Avenue, this is a good
choice for people with limited bud-
gets who want to be close to the
action. *327 Caribou St.* ☎ *403/762-
5134. www.bluemtnlodge.com. 10
units. Doubles $119–$179. MC, V.
Map p 76.*

**Buffalo Mountain Lodge** BANFF
With peeled log frames, feather
duvets over flannel sheets, fieldstone
fireplaces, and log furniture, there's
a preppy cottage feel to this collection of buildings on Tunnel Mountain.
It's one of the more classy places in
town, but maintains a casually elegant, outdoorsy feel. *700 Tunnel
Mountain Rd.* ☎ *800/661-1367 or
403/762-2400. www.crmr.com. 108
units. Doubles $259–$339. AE, MC, V.
Map p 76.*

**Buffaloberry Bed and Break-
fast** BANFF The unpretentious
owners of this little inn love the outdoors, and their B&B, in a building
nestled in one of downtown Banff's
quieter areas, may be the best sleep
in town, thanks to soundproof
rooms, blackout curtains, solid-core
doors, and luxurious natural linens.
Bathrooms are spacious. *417 Mar-
ten St.* ☎ *403/762-3750. www.
buffaloberry.com. 4 units. Doubles
$235–$325. Breakfast included. MC,
V. Map p 76.*

**Driftwood** BANFF If all you really
want is a comfortable and clean
place to sleep after spending the
days in the great mountains, this is
an undiscovered gem. Since it's
next door to the Ptarmigan Inn, and
has the same owners, guests have
use of the restaurant, hot tub, and
wireless at bargain prices. The beds
are super soft, and topped with

*Willow Stream Spa at the Fairmont Banff
Springs Hotel.*

fluffy duvets. *337 Banff Ave.* ☎ *800/
661-8310 or 403/762-4496. www.best
ofbanff.com/tdi. 32 units. Doubles
$184. AE, DISC, MC, V. Map p 76.*

★★ **Fairmont Banff Springs
Hotel** BANFF One of the most
famous buildings in Canada, this
spectacular hotel is a true experience. Rooms are notoriously small,
so don't plan to spend much time
indoors. The new Gold Floor has by
far the nicest rooms. The list of amenities, from the Willow Stream Spa,
to a bowling center, horse stables,
and nine restaurants, overwhelms.
This is an unforgettable place to
spend a few nights, but it doesn't
come cheap. Packages including
breakfasts and online specials will
help with the high price tag. *405
Spray Ave.* ☎ *800/441-1414 or
403/762-2211. www.fairmont.com/
banffsprings. 768 units. Doubles
$259, $739. AE, DC, DISC, MC, V.
Map p 76.*

★★ **Fairmont Chateau Lake
Louise** LAKE LOUISE The award-
winning landmark hotel is elegant,
with a Swiss Alpine feel, and more
comfortable than the Banff Springs.
Rooms with lake views are much
more than those on the other side
of the hall (which still have nice

*A room with a view of the lake at Fairmont Chateau Lake Louise.*

mountain views). A new Gold Floor offers superior service. The pool is nothing special, but the hotel's rich heritage, coupled with access to amazing hiking and skiing, is unmatched on the planet. *111 Lake Louise Dr.* ☎ *800/441-1414 or 403/ 522-3511. www.fairmont.com/lake louise. 554 units. Doubles $279–$599. AE, DISC, DC, MC, V. Map p 76.*

### kids Fox Hotel and Suites

BANFF    More contemporary than most of the hotels in town, rooms are mostly suites with kitchenettes and one or two bedrooms. Loft-style second-floor units have mountain views. The courtyard has a stunning hot pool themed after the historic Banff springs. *46 Banff Ave.* ☎ *800/ 661-8310 or 403/760-8500. www. bestofbanff.com/fox. 117 units. Doubles $269–$664. AE, DISC, MC, V. Map p 76.*

### Hidden Ridge Resort BANFF

If you'd like lots of personal space, and to be away from the bustle of Banff Avenue, this collection of styl- ish cabins along Tunnel Mountain Road provides privacy in town house–style apartments. In 2009, they added full kitchens and wood- burning fireplaces to all units, and two new outdoor hot pools with

fabulous views above Banff. *901 Hidden Ridge Way.* ☎ *800/661-1372 or 403/762-3544. www.bestofbanff. com/hrr. 107 units. Chalets $254– $559. AE, DISC, MC, V. Map p 76.*

### Johnston Canyon Campground

This is a tranquil campground nestled in a pleasant forest less than 20 min- utes from Banff Townsite. The nicest of the sites back onto Johnston Creek. *25km (16 miles) west of Banff Townsite on the Bow Valley Pkwy., Hwy. 1A. 132 sites. No RV hookups. Sites $27. AE, MC, V. Closed Sept 15–May 28.*

### Lake Louise Alpine Centre

LAKE LOUISE    Don't let the fact that this is a hostel turn you off a great value. Rooms range from small dor- mitories and simple doubles to larger rooms that sleep up to six. Simple communal bathrooms and showers are down the hall. *203 Vil- lage Rd.* ☎ *403/522-2201. www. hostellingintl.ca/alberta. 45 units. Dorms from $31–$117. MC, V. Map p 76.*

### Lake Louise Campground LAKE

LOUISE    This campground is down- hill from the Fairmont Chateau Lake Louise, away from the lake. The tent area is in the trees near the river. The trailer area is more open and closer to the highway and railway line. It's a 10-minute walk to Lake Louise Village. *58km (36 miles) northwest of Banff Townsite on the Trans-Canada Hwy. 1. Exit at Lake Louise and turn left after passing under the railway bridge onto Fairview Rd. Lake Louise Tent: 210 sites. No RV hookups. $28. Closed Sept 29–May 14. Lake Louise Trailer: 189 sites. Electrical hookups only. $32. Open year-round. Map p 76.*

**Num-Ti-Jah Lodge** ICEFIELDS PARKWAY    Banff's most scenic lodge is rustic, historic, and secluded. You'll pay for the location, not the amenities. The stairs creak as you climb them and the walls are thin. Rooms are clean, though quite basic. Heaps of character and history manage to cover up the need for a major upgrade. *40km (25 miles) north of Lake Louise on the Icefields Pkwy.* ☎ *403/522-2167. www. num-ti-jah.com. 25 units. Doubles $298–$427. AE, MC, V. Map p 76.*

**★★ Post Hotel** LAKE LOUISE    A quintessential and exquisite mountain inn, the Post Hotel combines beautiful guest rooms and excellent service in a peaceful location. Guest rooms are simple but luxurious, with fireplaces, down quilts, and heated

*A common area inside the Lake Louise Alpine Centre.*

slate floors in the bathrooms. The Temple Mountain Spa is the best in Lake Louise. *200 Pipestone.* ☎ *800/ 661-1586 or 403/522-3989. www. posthotel.com. 92 units. Doubles $345–$850. AE, MC, V. Map p 76.*

**Rimrock Resort Hotel** BANFF Modern and slick, the Rimrock has a great view and fine lodgings. The lobby is graced by a giant marble fireplace, cherry oak walls, leather chairs, and big windows offering views you can't get even in the penthouses of other local hotels.

*A bedroom inside the Fox Hotel & Suites.*

*A peaceful sitting room at the Post Hotel.*

Peaceful and elegant, rooms are airy, luxurious, and large. Request one on the east face of the south wing for the choicest views. *300 Mountain Ave.* ☎ *800/661-1587 or 403/762-3356. www.rimrockresort. com. 346 units. Doubles $318–$1,230. AE, DISC, MC, V. Map p 76.*

**Rundlestone Lodge** BANFF
There is a long line of mid-size hotels and motels along Banff Avenue. This one stands out for recent renovations that have given it a more modern feel. The gym, pool, and the large size of standard rooms add value. Predictable but clean, the service here is also very friendly. *537 Banff Ave.* ☎ *800/661-8630 or 403/762-2201. www.rundlestone.com. 96*

rooms. Doubles $188–$289. AE, DISC, MC, V. Map p 76.

**★★ Skoki Lodge** BACKCOUNTRY
This is a classic backcountry lodge built nearly a century ago, so you must ski or hike 11km (6.8 miles) to get here, arriving to a gorgeous valley behind the Lake Louise ski area. The lodge is rustic; there is no electricity or running water. There are, however, incredible trails at your doorstep and true Rocky Mountain seclusion. *Banff National Park.* ☎ *800/258-7669. www.skokilodge. com. From $194 per person including meals. AE, MC, V. Map p 76.*

**Storm Mountain Lodge** BANFF OUTSKIRTS    A collection of

*A room with a view at the Rimrock Resort Hotel.*

old-fashioned cabins halfway between Banff and Lake Louise have been nicely restored with large tubs, crackling fireplaces, and comfy beds. Unit nos. 9 and 10 are farthest from the sometimes-noisy Hwy. 93. Nos. 11 and 14 have great views of Castle Mountain. *On Hwy. 93 just west of Castle Junction.* ☎ *403/762-4155. www.stormmountainlodge.com. 14 units. Cabins $199–$289. MC, V. Map p 76.*

## Tunnel Mountain Village Campground

BANFF You can walk to Banff Avenue from the park's biggest campground. It's divided into three sections: a mixed tent and RV camp 2.5km (1½ miles) east of town; an RV mecca 4km (2½ miles) east of town; and a trailer- and tenter-friendly section to the east of the RV area. *4km (2½ miles) east of Banff Townsite on Tunnel Mountain Rd. Tunnel Mountain Village I: 618 sites. No RV hookups. $27. Closed Oct. 2–May 7. Tunnel Mountain Village II: 188 sites. Electrical hookups only. $32. AE, MC, V. Open year-round. Tunnel Mountain Trailer Court: 321 sites. Full hookups. $38. Closed Oct 2–May 7. AE, MC, V. Map p 76.*

## Two Jack Campground

MINNEWANKA LOOP There are two areas here. The main area (which is larger and busier) is just off the road in a densely wooded forest 13km (8 miles) northeast of Banff Townsite, on the Minnewanka Loop. It's quite private, although there are no great views. The second area is next to

*A campsite at Two Jack Campground.*

the lake and is very popular since it is the most scenic and peaceful campground near the Town of Banff. *12km (7½ miles) from Banff Townsite on Minnewanka Loop Rd. Two Jack Main: 380 sites. RV-friendly but no RV hookups. $22. Closed Sept 9–May 4. Two Jack Lakeside: 74 sites. No RV hookups. $27. Closed Sept 15–May 14. AE, MC, V. Map p 76.*

## Waterfowl Lake Campground

ICEFIELDS PARKWAY This is my favorite in the park because of the scenery and peacefulness. There is an open area on the lakeshore for relaxing or playing games, plus amazing views of the surrounding mountains and glaciers. *57km (35 miles) north of Lake Louise on the Icefields Pkwy., Hwy. 93. 116 sites. No RV hookups. $22. Closed Sept 8–June 18. No credit cards. Map p 76.*

Banff National Park

# Banff **Shopping & Nightlife**

0 ——— 1/4 mi
0 ——— .25 km

● ● ● Walking Path

**Arts and Entertainment**
Banff Alpine Lights at
    Sulphur Mountain 22
The Banff Centre 21
Bowling at Fairmont
    Banff Springs 23
Evening Wildlife Safari 7
Lux Theatre 4
Oh Canada Eh
    Dinner Theatre 2

**Nightlife**
Aurora Nightclub 20
The Banff Rose and Crown 12
The Bison Lounge 9
Buffalo Paddock 14
Hoodoo Lounge 11
The Outpost 1
Saint James's Gate 5
Tommy's Neighbouhood
    Pub 19
Wild Bill's Legendary
    Saloon 10

**Shopping**
Banff Wine Store 13
The Bay 15
The Bear and Butterfly 8
Chocolaterie Bernard
    Callebaut 17
Lammle's Western Wear
    and Tack 3
Monod's 16
Philippe of Banff 18
Qiviuk 24
Roots 6

# Shopping & Nightlife Best Bets

Best **Canadiana Souvenirs**
The Bay, *125 Banff Ave. (p 87)*

Best **Cowboy Culture**
Wild Bill's, *201 Banff Ave. (p 90)*;
and Lammle's Cascade Plaza, *317
Banff Ave. (p 54)*

Best **Dance Floor**
Aurora, *110 Banff Ave (p 89)*

Best **Eco-Gifts**
The Bear and Butterfly, *214 Banff
Ave. (p 86)*

Best **Family Night Out**
Oh Canada Eh Dinner Theatre, *125
Kananaskis Way, Canmore (p 89)*

Best **Outdoor Gear**
Monod's, *129 Banff Ave. (p 87)*

Best **for Singles**
Hoodoo, *137 Banff Ave. (p 89)*

Best **Jazz**
Banff Centre, *107 Tunnel Mountain
Rd.. (p 88)*

Best **Low-Key Après Ski**
Tommy's Neighbourhood Pub, *120
Banff Ave. (p 90)*

Best **Selection of Beer on Tap**
Saint James's Gate, *205 Wolf St.
(p 90)*

Best **Wine and Tapas**
The Bison Lounge, *213 Bear St.
(p 89)*

Best **View**
★★ Fairmont Chateau Lake Louise, *111 Lake Louise Dr. (p 62)*

*Cowboy hats at Lammle's Western Wear.*

# Shopping, Arts & Nightlife A to Z

## Shopping

**Banff Wine Store** BANFF   The staff at this basement-level shop is incredibly knowledgeable and friendly. Ask for tips on a post-hike pinot or an après-ski cabernet. There are labels from more than a dozen countries and a wide price range, including Canadian ice wine. They also deliver to your hotel! *302 Caribou St.* ☎ *403/782-3465. AE, MC, V. Map p 84.*

**The Bay** BANFF   The Hudson's Bay Company is a Canadian institution established in 1670. Today, The Bay sells everything from cosmetics to Cuisinarts in their three-level department store. Souvenirs here include maple candies, the famous Hudson's Bay blankets, and Olympic uniforms. *125 Banff Ave.* ☎ *403/762-5525. AE, DC, DISC, MC, V. Map p 84.*

**The Bear and Butterfly** BANFF   Nature-oriented items like maps, guidebooks, books on local history, and wildlife guides are the main focus at both this Banff Avenue shop and its sister location inside the Banff Information Centre. Many local artists are showcased here as well. Proceeds fund educational programs run by the Friends of Banff National Park. *214 Banff Ave.* ☎ *403/762-8911. AE, MC, V. Map p 84.*

**Chocolaterie Bernard Callebaut** BANFF   This Belgian-born Calgarian is a fifth-generation chocolate maker who says he eats at least six different chocolates each day. His Banff store, inside the Harmony Lane mall, is practically an education in all things chocolate. Choose from 48 flavors, including dark chocolate–coated ginger, ganache cream, and truffles. *111 Banff Ave.* ☎ *403/762-4106. AE, MC, V. Map p 84.*

**Lammle's Western Wear and Tack** BANFF   For true-blue cowboy gear, head upstairs in Cascade Plaza. Start with a Shady Brady cowboy hat and a pair of Wrangler jeans with a

*Art on display at the The Bear & Butterfly.*

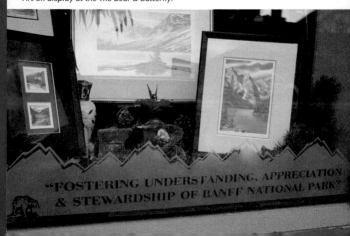

"FOSTERING UNDERSTANDING, APPRECIATION & STEWARDSHIP OF BANFF NATIONAL PARK"

*Some of the delectables for sale at Chocolaterie Bernard Callebaut.*

silver belt; then wrap up the whole outfit up with a pair of Dan Post cowboy boots. They also have kidswear for junior saddle ropers. *Cascade Plaza, 317 Banff Ave.* ☎ *403/762-5460. AE, MC, V. Map p 84.*

**Monod's** BANFF   Banff's oldest outdoor clothing and equipment retailer is a busy, jam-packed shop staffed by keen outdoorsy types. Hiking boots are upstairs at the back, along with fly-fishing rods, while climbing harnesses and tents are downstairs, and cold-weather wear right in the middle. Fleeces anyone? *129 Banff Ave.* ☎ *403/762-4571. AE, MC, V. Map p 84.*

**Philippe of Banff** BANFF   Since Banff is the jewel of the Rockies, it's only appropriate that you'd find some diamonds at this fine jeweler's atelier. Banff goldsmith Philippe Plourde handcrafts stunning jewelry that honors tradition yet embraces modern styles. *130 Banff Ave.* ☎ *403/760-8744. AE, MC, V. Map p 84.*

**Qiviuk** BANFF   Celebrities have discovered that it's softer than cashmere, warmer than beaver or fox fur, lighter than wool. The supple and plush pelt from the Canadian Arctic musk ox comes from the Far North, making qiviuk the world's

rarest natural fiber. This store in the Banff Springs sells sweaters, coats, hats, shawls and scarves. *Fairmont Banff Springs Hotel, 405 Spray Ave.* ☎ *403/762-4460. AE, DC, MC, V. Map p 84.*

**Roots** BANFF   Canada's iconic leather and casual clothing shop is a great place for a maple-leaf–inspired souvenir, from hoodies to baby sleepers. They've lately started dabbling in yoga wear and linens, but maintain their—um, roots—with sweats. This is your chance to adapt the Canadian lifestyle with genuine leather and always-stylish purses, jackets, and shoes. *277 Banff Ave.* ☎ *403/762-9434. AE, MC, V. Map p 84.*

### Arts & Entertainment
**Banff Alpine Lights at Sulphur Mountain** BANFF   Ride the Sulphur Mountain Gondola on Saturday nights during summertime and combine it with an unforgettable "Prime Rib Prime View" dinner way, way above the lights of town. *At the end of Mountain Rd., 2.5km (1½ miles) from Banff Ave.* ☎ *403/762-2523. www.explorerockies.com. Sat only June 13–Oct 10 5–9pm. Adults $47, kids $26. Map p 84.*

*Outerwear for sale at Monod's.*

### ★★★ The Banff Centre BANFF

For inspiring concerts featuring world-class jazz, dance, pop, folk, and world music, keep an eye on the calendar and hope something is happening during your visit. *St. Julien Rd.* ☎ *403/762-6301. www. banffcentre.ca. Wed, Fri, Sat, and Sun 9pm–2am. Admission varies. Map p 84.*

### kids Bowling at Fairmont Banff Springs BANFF There are

four lanes of five-pin bowling at the Fairmont Banff Springs Hotel, which makes for a lively and fun family evening activity, especially on a stormy night. There's also a video game arcade and bar inside. *405 Spray Ave., in the Conference Centre.* ☎ *403/762-6892. www.fairmont. com/banffsprings. Lanes $45/hour. Mon–Thurs 4–10pm, Fri noon–midnight, Sat 10am–midnight, Sun noon–11pm. Map p 84.*

### ★ Evening Wildlife Safari

BANFF    Two-hour van-based wildlife tours run by Discover Banff Tours depart Banff each evening, taking full advantage of what is perhaps your best bet for wildlife sightings. The guides are very good, and binoculars are provided. *Discover Banff Tours' office is in Sundance Mall, 215 Banff Ave.* ☎ *403/760-5007. www.banfftours.com. Daily at 6:30pm. Adults $39, kids 5–12 $25. Map p 84.*

### Lux Theatre BANFF    Banff's ven-

erable cinema plays mainly first-run Hollywood hits, although there are occasional showings of more outdoorsy films from the Banff Mountain Film Festival competition. *229 Bear St.* ☎ *403/762-8595. Adults $10, children under 12 $7. Map p 84.*

*Souvenirs on display at The Bay.*

*Dancers perform at The Banff Centre.*

### Oh Canada Eh Dinner Theatre
CANMORE    With lumberjacks, voyageurs, Mounties, and a bunch of Canadian hits, this is a fun night of singing, dancing, and general Canuck-teasing. Dinner is served family-style at long tables. *125 Kananaskis Way, Canmore.* ☎ *800/773-0004 or 403/609-0004. www. ohcanadaeh.com. Fri–Wed starting at 6:15pm. Adults $63, kids 16 and under free with an adult or $29. Map p 84.*

## Nightlife
### Aurora Nightclub BANFF   The
best spot for later-night dancing and funky techno atmosphere. There's a cigar room, a martini bar, and karaoke on Thursdays. *110 Banff Ave., downstairs.* ☎ *403/760-5300. www. aurorabanff.com. Admission varies $6-$12. Map p 84.*

### The Banff Rose and Crown
BANFF   With a spacious rooftop patio and a long list of beers on tap, this is a laid-back favorite with a low-brow style. There is often live music, including Maritime Mondays for fans of the east coast. *202 Banff Ave., upstairs.* ☎ *403/762-2121. www. roseandcrown.ca. Admission varies $4-$12. Daily 11am–2am. Map p 84.*

### ★★ The Bison Lounge BANFF
A great selection of wine by the glass and snacks from the outstanding bistro upstairs (p 70) makes this appealing for the more cosmopolitan and stylish crowd. Check the chalkboard tasting specials, and grab a spot at the communal table to make new friends. *213 Bear St.* ☎ *403/762-5550. www.thebison.ca. Mon–Fri 11am–1am; Sat–Sun noon–2am. Map p 84.*

### Buffalo Paddock BANFF   On
the top floor of the Mount Royal Hotel, come for billiards, darts, shuffleboard, foosball, and more than a dozen large-screen TVs. *138 Banff Ave.* ☎ *403/760-8543. Free admission. Daily noon–2am. Map p 84.*

### Hoodoo Lounge BANFF   Those
who really want to party can join the young crowd in the basement here for top-20 dance tunes. Specials practically every night of the week, from ladies' night to live music. *137 Banff Ave.* ☎ *403/760-8636. www. hoodoolounge.com. Admission varies $5-$14. Daily 9pm–2am; closed Wed and Sun. Map p 84.*

### The Outpost LAKE LOUISE   The
best spot for an evening drink in Lake Louise is in the basement pub beneath the Post Hotel for draft beer and light pub food similar to

*The bar at Aurora Nightclub.*

the gourmet stuff on offer upstairs. *200 Pipestone.* ☎ *403/522-3989. Free admission. Daily 4:30pm–midnight. Map p 84.*

★ **Saint James's Gate** BANFF Inspired by the birthplace of Guinness, selecting a draught here is just about the toughest challenge in Banff—there are 33 beers on tap, as well as 50 single-malt scotches and 10 Irish whiskeys. Live music is almost always Celtic, and a blast. *205 Wolf St.* ☎ *403/762-9355. www. stjamesgatebanff.com. Admission varies, $4-$14. Daily 11am–2am. Map p 84.*

**Tommy's Neighbourhood Pub** BANFF Locals here are happy to share stories of what it's like to live in such a storied town. This is a friendly place where you can actually have a conversation without yelling. *120 Banff Ave.* ☎ *403/762-8888. www.tommysneighbourhood pub.com. Free admission. Daily 11am–2am. Map p 84.*

★ **Wild Bill's Legendary Saloon** BANFF The local cowboy hangout is fun and not necessarily all about the yee-haw. What can I say? Head here if you want to drink beer and do some line dancing. Wednesday nights brings line-dance lessons. *201 Banff Ave., upstairs.* ☎ *403/762-0333. www.wbsaloon.com. Admission varies, $5-$18. Daily 11am–2am. Map p 84.* ●

The Canadian Rockies

# Kananaskis Country

0         10 mi
0         10 km

*Ghost River Wilderness*

CASCADE MTN.

✈ Mt. Norquay

Lake Minnewanka

1A

Banff

1

Park Gate

To Calgary ↗

1A

MT. RUNDLE

Exshaw

Seebe

BANFF NATIONAL PARK

Canmore

Bow Valley Prov. Park

ALBERTA
BRITISH COLUMBIA

Spray River

Bow Valley Wildland Provincial Park

Mt. Assiniboine Provincial Park

Spray Lakes Reservoir

BULLER MOUNTAIN

Kananaskis Village

MT. ASSINIBOINE

Marvel Lake

Spray Valley Provincial Park

742

Fortress Mountain

Elbow-Sheep Wildland Provincial Park

Peter Lougheed Provincial Park

40

MT. SIR DOUGLAS

Kananaskis Lakes

### Legend

△ Campground
⛽ Gasoline
✚ Hospital/First Aid
ⓘ Information
▲ Mountain
■ Point of Interest
✈ Ski Resort

1 Barrier Lake Visitors Centre
2 Nakiska
3 Kananaskis Village
4 Fireweed Grill
5 Kananaskis Country Golf Course
6 Peter Lougheed Visitors Centre

### Area of map inset

Edmonton
ALBERTA
16
40
16
2
Jasper
BRITISH COLUMBIA
93
Lake Louise
Golden
1
Banff
Calgary
2
**Area of map**
CANADA
UNITED STATES

*Previous Page: Hiking on the Skyline Trail with Mount Edith-Cavell in the background.*

**K**ananaskis Country is a vast area of rugged mountain wilderness that contains four provincial parks and "multiple-use" land where forestry, cattle-grazing, and petroleum development are permitted. From the golf courses to the trails, things are quiet here compared to Banff, drawing mainly weekenders from Calgary. Kananaskis is named for a Cree native who was reportedly struck by an axe but survived, and there's a good variety of outdoor activities, gorgeous scenery, and excellent infrastructure. **START: Banff.**

The chair lift at Nakiska ski resort.

From Banff, take the Trans-Canada Highway west 55km (34 miles). Turn south on Hwy. 40, the Kananaskis Trail.

**❶ Barrier Lake Visitors Centre.** This is a good first stop, at the entrance to Kananaskis Country on Hwy. 40. Pick up brochures and maps. ⏲ *15 mins. Hwy. 40, 8km (5 miles) south of Trans-Canada Hwy. 1.* ☎ *403/673-3985. Mid-June to mid-Sept daily 8am–6pm; mid-Sept to mid-June Mon–Thurs 9am–4pm, Sat and Sun 9am–5pm.*

**Continue south on Hwy. 40 for 14km (8⅔ miles). Turn right towards Kananaskis Village, continuing straight for 2.5km (1½ miles).**

**❷ Nakiska.** The site of the alpine skiing events at the 1988 Calgary Winter Olympics, this is a great family ski hill, steps from Kananaskis Village on the lower slopes of Mount Allan. Pop by for a photo-op beside assorted Olympic paraphernalia. *2.5km (1½ miles) from Kananaskis Village on Village Rd.* ☎ *403/591-7777. www.skinakiska.com.*

**Return back towards Hwy. 40, turning right after 2.5km (1½ miles).**

The Kananaskis Country Golf Course.

*Mount Kidd and wetlands in Peter Lougheed Provincial Park.*

**3 Kananaskis Village.** The heart of "K-Country" is home to a golf course, tennis courts, hotels, horse-riding stables, a cafe, plenty of trails, and a ski resort. It's a year-round resort hub that offers a pleasant stroll and a handful of shops. *26km (16 miles) south of Trans-Canada Hwy. 1 on Hwy. 40. Turn right on Mount Allen Dr. and left on Centennial Dr. Follow directions to parking lot.*

Pop into the Delta Lodge at Kananaskis for lunch at the **4 Fireweed Grill**. On a summer day, sit on the patio. There are plenty of pizzas and salads to choose from, but I suggest the indulgent Alberta beef dip,

famous in these parts. *1 Centennial Dr., Kananaskis Village.* ☎ *403/591-6272. $$.*

**Head north out of the Village and then turn left at the first stop sign.**

**5 Kananaskis Country Golf Course.** Two 18-hole, par-72 courses make up one of the top-rated and most scenic golf resorts in Canada. *Clubhouse is on Lorette Dr. south of Kananaskis Village.* ☎ *877/591-2525 or 403/591-7272; www.kananaskisgolf.com. Green fees $81. Open 7am-10pm, early May-mid Oct.*

**Continue south on Hwy. 40 for 30km (19 miles), turn west on Kananaskis Lakes Trail and travel 3.7km (2⅓ miles).**

**6 Peter Lougheed Provincial Park.** Easy interpretive trails lead out from an excellent visitors centre onto the shores of the lovely Upper and Lower Kananaskis Lakes. A more demanding hike goes up from the peninsula in between the two lakes to Mount Indefatigable for superb valley views (hiking boots a must!). Mountain bikers come for the Pocaterra Trail. ☎ *403/591-6322. June–Sept daily 9am–8pm; Oct–May Mon–Thurs 9:30am–4:30pm and Fri–Sat 9am–5pm.*

## Chinook Country

**Don't be surprised by quick and drastic rises in temperatures** during wintertime here. When warm Pacific air comes funneling through to the foothills and slams into a cold high pressure air mass, dry air is compressed and heated, dropping quickly and producing a phenomenon known as a chinook. Local temperatures can go up as much as 40°C (72°F) in 20 minutes. Most winters bring 20 chinook days a year to the eastern edge of the Canadian Rockies near Kananaskis Country.

# Canmore

1. Grassi Lakes
2. Coffee Mine
3. Canmore Geoscience Museum
4. Avens Gallery
5. Bow River Walk
6. Harvest
7. Canmore Nordic Centre Provincial Park

••• Walking Path

I t's hard to beat Canmore. The town of 12,000 boasts beautiful scenery, world-class trails, plus a relatively short commute to Banff or Calgary. Mountains rise high in all directions, and the turquoise Bow River flows through town. Locals take pride in healthy living, the great cafes and restaurants, and the keen arts scene that have earned Canmore the nickname of "Alberta's Aspen." Many visitors stay here for hotel rates that are typically lower than in Banff, making it a good place to begin day trips into the park. The best way to explore Canmore is on foot. START: **Downtown Canmore.**

At the west end of Main Street, turn left and drive over the Bow River. Turn left again at Three Sisters Drive and right onto Spray Lakes Road. One kilometer (2/3 mile) past the Nordic Centre, turn left into a parking lot for the trail head.

1 ★★ **Grassi Lakes.** Start the day with a moderate, short but stunning hike just above town. It's a

4km (2.5-mile) loop that takes you up historic steps, past a waterfall and on to two small, jewel-like lakes. *Just past Nordic Centre on the Smith Dorrien-Spray Lakes Rd.*

Head back down the hill, around the shore of the reservoir, and into town. Park in the lot behind 8th Street and between the Library and Information Centre.

# Extreme Golf in the Rockies

There are three outstanding golf courses at Canmore. The oldest course in town is the friendly 18-hole **Canmore Golf and Curling Club** (2000 8th Ave.; ☎ 403/678-4785; www.canmoregolf.net) close to downtown, along the Bow River. Greens fees are $80 per person. The clubhouse has one of the best patios in town. On the north side of Canmore is **SilverTip Resort** (1000 SilverTip Trail, exit at the main Canmore exit and take first left before the lights; ☎ 877/877-5444 or 403/678-1600; www.silvertipresort.com). Calling what it offers "extreme mountain golf," this Les Furber–designed 18-hole, par-72 course is one of a kind. Greens fees range from $150 to $175. **Stewart Creek Golf Course** (1 Stewart Creek Rd., via the Three Sisters Pkwy. exit just east of Canmore; ☎ 877/993-4653 or 403/609-6099; www.stewartcreekgolf.com) is another "high mountain" course that winds along the picturesque lower slopes of the Three Sisters Mountain on the south side of the Bow Valley. Greens fees range from $150 to $195.

**2 Coffee Mine**. Reward yourself with breakfast on Main Street. There are many places to choose from, but the baked goods and deluxe breakfast sandwiches at this newly upgraded favorite are real standouts. *103-802 Main St., on 7th Ave.* ☎ *403/678-2241. Daily 9am–4pm. $.*

**In front, across 7th Avenue and just to the left of you is:**

**3 Canmore Geoscience Museum.** From coal mining to Olympic fame, there's human as well as geological history to discover in this museum, housed in Canmore's new Civic Centre, which has won awards for its eco-friendly design. *902b 7th Ave.* ☎ *403/678-2462. www.cmags.org. Admission $3 adults, $2 students and seniors. Summer Mon–Tues noon–5pm, Wed–Sat 10am–6pm; Sept 5–May 17 Mon–Fri noon–5pm, Sat–Sun 11am–5pm.*

*A cyclist crosses a bridge over the Bow River.*

*A grilled sandwich from Harvest.*

**Stroll to the left along Main Street for window shopping. On the south side is the:**

④ **Avens Gallery.** For 20 years, this has been the premier art gallery in Canmore. There's small art (jewelry, sculpture, blown glass), but the most impressive are the large canvases representing the inspiring local scenery. *104-709 Main St.* ☎ *403/678-4471. Wed–Sun 11am–5pm.*

**Continue down Main Street and keep straight as Main Street becomes Riverview Place. At the far end of the cul-de-sac, a sign marks the beginning of a walking trail.**

⑤ **Bow River Walk.** At the end of Main Street, follow footpath signs to the Bow River Walk, which traces both sides of this turquoise alpine river while taking in dazzling mountain scenery. A gentle 30-minute loop takes you over the old railway bridge, past the TransAlta Plant, and back to town over Bridge Road.

**Return to Main Street, turning left on 7th Avenue and right on 10th Street.**

⑥ ★ **Harvest.** This is where locals grab a healthy lunch. Most sandwiches are grilled, croque monsieur–style. On Sundays, there are homemade cinnamon buns. It's just off Main Street. *718 10th St.* ☎ *403/678-3747. Mon–Fri 8am–4pm, Sun 10am–3pm. $.*

**Get back in the car and retrace your route up towards Grassi Lakes. Take a right at the large signs.**

⑦ **Canmore Nordic Centre Provincial Park.** The park was the host of the Nordic skiing and biathlon events for the 1988 Calgary Winter Olympics, and is the only Canadian stop on the Nordic World Cup tour. There are more than 65km (40 miles) of ski trails in winter, 100km (62 miles) of mountain-bike trails in summer, and a Frisbee golf course. *1.8km/1 mile south of Canmore, take Rundle Dr. across the Bow River Bridge, go left at Three Sisters Dr, and right at Spray Lakes Rd.; follow signs.* ☎ *403/678-2400.*

*A skier at the Canmore Nordic Centre.*

The Canadian Rockies

# Icefields Parkway (Jasper)

0    10 mi
0    10 km

Hinton

Area of map

ALBERTA

Edmonton

Jasper

Lake Louise

Golden

Banff

Calgary

BRITISH COLUMBIA

CANADA
UNITED STATES

Brule Lake

Indian River

Park Gate

Snaring River Campground

Pyramid Lake
Patricia Lake
Lake Annette

Jasper

Medicine Lake

Wapiti Campground

Ski Marmot Basin

Whistlers Campground
Wabasso Campground

JASPER NATIONAL PARK

Maligne River

Maligne Lake

MOUNT EDITH CAVELL

MOUNT CHRISTIE

Athabasca River

Icefields

Sunwapta River

Chaba Icefield

Columbia Icefield

To Lake Louise, Banff

| | Campground |
| | Hospital/First Aid |
| | Information |
| | Mountain |
| | Point of Interest |
| | Ski Area |

1   The Columbia Icefield
2   The Glacier Experience
3   Tangle Falls Viewpoint
4   Sunwapta Falls
5   Highway 93A
6   Athabasca Falls
7   Cavell Road
8   Mount Edith Cavell
9   Path of the Glacier Trail

**A**s you drive north on the Icefields Parkway, Hwy. 93, you enter Jasper National Park, the largest of the national parks in the Canadian Rockies at 10,878 sq. km (4,200 sq. miles). Large carnivores roam the wide valleys here, so drive slowly and keep an eye out for wildlife; the scenery sometimes more closely resembles the moon than the Rocky Mountains. This tour only covers the highway north of the Icefields Centre; for information on the southern half of the Parkway, see p 64. START: **Icefields Centre, 125km (78 miles) north of Lake Louise and 105km (65 miles) south of Jasper Townsite.**

**①** ★★★ **The Columbia Icefield.** The geographical heart of the Icefields Parkway is a world-class natural wonder and living laboratory that examines glaciology and mountain geology. It's fantastically visitor friendly, and is located just north of the Banff National Park border, some 103km (64 miles) south of the Town of Jasper. The Icefields Centre, open May 1 to mid-October, is staffed by Parks Canada. ☎ *780/852-6288.*

**②** ★★ **The Glacier Experience.** The venerable Brewster family operates giant "snocoaches" that take you right on to the Athabasca Glacier, giving you a sense of the enormity of this icefield. You get about 15 minutes to walk on top of the 300m–thick (984-ft.) sheets of ice. Although coaches leave every 15 minutes, the tours can be very busy, especially in summer, so reservations are highly recommended. ☎ *403/762-6735. www. explorerockies.com. Adults $47, kids*

*6–15 $23. Apr 10–30 and Oct 1–18 10am–4pm; May 1–31 and Sept 1–30 9am–5pm; June 1–Aug 31 9am–6pm.*

**Drive north on the Icefields Parkway for 9km (5½ miles).**

**③** ★ **Tangle Falls Viewpoint.** Just off the west side of the highway at the top of a broad turn are views of the Stutfield Glacier. This is also one of the best chances in the Canadian Rockies to see mountain goats close up, who are drawn to mineral licks on both sides of the road. *96km (60 miles) from Jasper and 9km (5½ miles) from the Icefields Centre. Map p 98.*

**Continue north on the Icefields Parkway for 41km (25 miles).**

**④** **Sunwapta Falls.** The Sunwapta River tumbles through a steep-walled limestone gorge, making a sharp turn from northwest to southwest. Follow a 2km (1.2-mile)

*Mount Athabasca at the Columbia Icefields.*

*An aerial view of Sunwapta Falls.*

trail along the north bank of the river for excellent views. *50km (31 miles) north of Icefields Centre and 55km (34 miles) south of Jasper Townsite. Follow turnoff to parking lot.*

**Continue north on the Icefields Parkway, turning northwest or left onto:**

**⑤ Hwy. 93A.** The Icefields Parkway soon meets Hwy. 93A, a scenic road with less traffic that heads up towards Jasper. It's a good option if you have time. *30km (19 miles) from Jasper and 75km (47 miles) from Icefields Centre.*

**Make a quick left into the parking lot at:**

**⑥ ★ Athabasca Falls.** The milky-blue Athabasca River pours through a narrow canyon cut out of quartzite rock. A nearby bridge offers phenomenal views of the thundering falls and Mount Kerkeslin in the background. *Just past the 93A turnoff, on south side of road, 30km (19 miles) south of Jasper and 75km (47 miles) north of the Icefields Centre.*

**Continue northwest on 93A. After 8km (5 miles), turn left.**

**⑦ ★ Cavell Road.** Follow Hwy. 93A north along the west bank of the Athabasca River and over the Whirlpool River to Cavell Road. Turn left. Completed in 1924, this narrow, winding road is challenging to drive, and is off-limits to most RVs and trailers (anything over 7m/23 ft.). It is also closed from October through June, depending on snow.

**⑧ Mount Edith Cavell.** At 3,363m (11,033 ft.), Mount Edith Cavell, named after a World War I heroine, is the highest and arguably most scenic mountain in the vicinity of Jasper Townsite. Angel Glacier saddles the northeastern slope and sends a tongue of ice off the cliffside. *28km (17 miles) from Hwy 93A on the Cavell Rd.*

**⑨ ★★ The Path of the Glacier Trail.** From the parking lot at the base of Mount Edith Cavell, this trail takes you over boulders, shrubbery, pebbles, and sand through a landscape which, less than a century ago, was covered by a glacier. New plants, trees, shrubs, and wildflowers have slowly returned to the area, known as a terminal moraine. *It's an easy 1.6km (1-mile) loop that will take 45 min.*

**Drive back down the Cavell Road and turn left on Hwy. 93A, which will take you back to Jasper.**

*Mount Edith Cavell.*

# Maligne Valley Road

0 ___ 10 mi
0 ___ 10 km

**JASPER NATIONAL PARK**

Pyramid Lake
Patricia Lake
Lake Annette
Jasper
Wapiti Campground
Whistlers Campground
Ski Marmot Basin
Medicine Lake
Maligne River
Maligne Lake
MOUNT EDITH CAVELL
Athabasca River
Icefields Parkway

**Area of map**

ALBERTA
Edmonton
Jasper
Golden
Lake Louise
Calgary
Banff
BRITISH COLUMBIA
CANADA
UNITED STATES

❶ Maligne Canyon
❷ Maligne Lake Cruise
   to Spirit Island
❸ Curly Phillips' Boathouse
❹ Mary Schaffer Loop

**T**his road takes you through the **Maligne Valley** and ends at the picturesque Maligne Lake. Wildlife can often be spotted on this half-day outing, including bighorn sheep, deer, elk, moose, grizzly bear, and black bear. With a handful of stops, some short hikes, and a boat cruise, it will take you most of the day. START: **Town of Jasper.**

**Drive east on Connaught Street, turning left onto Hwy. 16. After 4km (2.5 miles), turn south onto Maligne Lake Road.**

❶ **Maligne Canyon.** A spectacular example of the cutting power of moving water, this is a very long, gradual waterfall through a deep limestone canyon. There are a series of bridges that take you back and forth down the canyon. *2.3km (1.4 miles) on the Maligne Lake Road to Sixth Bridge parking lot.*

*Looking down at Maligne Canyon.*

Continue on the Maligne Lake Road to its end.

**2** ★★ kids **Maligne Lake Cruise to Spirit Island.** This is the best boat tour in the Canadian Rockies. From the deck of the glass-enclosed boats (which are heated on chilly days), watch for eagles, mountain goats, and even the odd avalanche. The cruise makes a stop halfway up the lake at the mysterious Spirit Island, then returns to the dock. *At the end of Maligne Lake Rd.* ☎ *866/625-4463 or 780/852-3370. www.malignelake.com. $55 adults, $27 kids 5–14. Cruises depart hourly in summer 10am–5pm.*

**3** **Curly Phillips' Boathouse.** Curly Phillips, a canoe guide and trapper from Ontario, built a floating boathouse on Maligne Lake in 1928 that still stands today. Rent canoes at this historic building for $30 an hour. *Just east of the cafeteria behind the first parking lot on Maligne Lake.* ☎ *780/852-3370.*

**4** **Mary Schaffer Loop.** (also known as Loop Trail) A pleasant hike around the north side of Maligne Lake, the largest lake in the Canadian Rockies, reaches a viewpoint with an interpretive display about explorer Mary Schaffer, the first woman of European descent to set eyes on the lake, in 1908, and the most prolific writer about the place. It's a 3.2km (2-mile) loop that will take you just over an hour.

# East of Jasper

**Miette Hot Springs.** ★ Head out for one of Jasper's best hikes (the Sulphur Skyline), then soak your tired bones in these hot mineral pools. From Jasper Townsite, follow the Yellowhead Hwy. 16, 42km (26 miles) east to Miette Road. Follow Miette Road 17km (11 miles) south to the end of the road. ☎ *780/866-3939. Admission $6 adults, $5.15 seniors and children, $18 family pass. Mid-May to 3rd week of June and early Sept to mid-Oct daily 10:30am–9pm; late June to early Sept daily 8:30am–10:30pm. Closed mid-Oct to mid-May.*

*A mineral pool at Miette Hot Springs.*

# Town of Jasper

| | Hospital/First Aid |
| | Parking |

1 Jasper National Park
  Information Centre
2 Heritage Railway Station
3 Jasper Tramway
4 Patricia St. Deli
5 Jasper –Yellowhead Museum
6 Old Fort Point
7 Pyramid and Patricia Lakes

0        1/4 mi
0        .25 km

To Banff

**L**ocated in the heart of the park, the town of Jasper came into being in anticipation of a transcontinental railway that now runs up the Athabasca Valley and through the Yellowhead Pass. The Canadian National Railway built a series of cabins on the shores of Lac Beauvert, which later became the Jasper Park Lodge. Today, the town feels very different from the Town of Banff—it's less crowded, and lacks the swanky shops and nightclubs of its southern counterpart. START: **Jasper Information Centre.**

**1 Jasper National Park Information Centre.** In this cozy and central heritage building, get your bearings and get information from the Friends of Jasper, Parks Canada, and Jasper Tourism and Commerce, all of which have booths at the information center. Jasper Tourism and Commerce can tell you about hotel, restaurant, and outfitting options in the park (☎ 780/852-3858). *500 Connaught Dr.* ☎ *780/852-6176.*

*Daily Apr 4–June 12 and Oct 1–31 9am–5pm; June 13–Aug 31 8:30am–7pm, Sept 1–30 9am–6pm and Nov 1–Apr 4 9am–4pm.*

**Cross Connaught Street to visit the:**

**2 Heritage Railway Station.** Like the CIBC Bank building next to the Info Centre, this building is a great example of the rustic Arts and Crafts architecture of its era. Built in 1921 and designated a Heritage Site in 1991, it now houses park administration as well as the train station. You can still picture Victorian ladies with their parasols and elaborate dresses mixing with rough 'n' tumble gold diggers at this old frontier outpost. In fact, many people still arrive in Jasper here via the ViaRail passenger train. *607 Connaught Dr.*

**Drive south 4km (2½ miles) from the townsite, on Hwy. 93A, turn west at Whistlers Road and continue for 2.5km (1½ miles) to the Tramway terminal, following clearly marked signs to:**

③ ★★ kids **Jasper Tramway.** Your quickest and easiest way to the high alpine terrain, this 7-minute gondola ride takes you up 973m (3,192 ft.), just short of the summit of the Whistlers. From the top, the views of the Athabasca and Miette valleys are stunning. There's a well-marked, though quite steep, 45-minute trail to the summit of the mountain. The view is more outstanding with each step upward. Dress warmly and wear comfortable

*The Jasper National Park Information Centre.*

walking shoes. At the summit, the panoramic view takes in six mountain ranges, including Mount Robson, the highest point in the Canadian Rockies. Rides leave every 10 minutes or so. ☎ 780/852-3093. *www.jaspertramway.com. $28 adults, $14 children under 15, free for children 4 and under. May 20–June 22 daily 9:30am–6:30pm; June 23–Aug 26 9am–8pm; Aug 27–Oct 8 10am–5pm. Closed mid-Oct to mid-May.*

## Travel Tip

Evenings in the Rockies are particularly enchanting, when the mountains take on the rose-colored glow known as "alpenglow." In the summer, the last trip down the mountain departs at 8:30pm.

**Return to town by the same route. Park on Patricia Street.**

④ **Patricia St. Deli.** The best sandwiches—and some of the friendliest people—in Jasper are at this deli right in the heart of town. "Two slices of bread with heaven in between," they say. A hiker's lunch includes chips and cookies for $13 and makes a great picnic. *606 Patricia St.* ☎ *780/852-4814. $.*

**Turn left on Pyramid Avenue and left again on Pyramid Lake Road.**

⑤ **Jasper–Yellowhead Museum.** Good for a rain day, this museum has exhibits with artifacts from the park's early days, including fur-trade and mountaineering equipment. You'll find legendary guide Curly Phillips's hand-built cedar-strip canoe, Métis beaded deerskin jackets, and the gear used during the first ascent of Mount Alberta in 1925. *400 Pyramid Lake Rd.* ☎ *780/852-3013. www.jaspermuseum.org.*

*Patricia Street.*

*$5 adults; $4 seniors, students, and children 6–18; free for children 5 and under. Daily 10am–9pm in summer. In winter, closed Mon–Wed.*

**Drive 5 minutes south of Jasper Townsite via Hwy 93A or Hazel Avenue, crossing Hwy. 16. Turn east on**

*View from Old Fort Point.*

**Old Fort Point Road and park in the first parking lot after the bridge.**

**6 ★★ Old Fort Point.** Climbing the stairs up Old Fort Point is steep, but worthwhile. Jutting out into the Athabasca River, the point offers great views that take in Jasper Townsite, Lac Beauvert, and the Fairmont Jasper Park Lodge. From here you can also catch sight of Mounts Kerkeslin and Hardisty to the southeast, and the snowy triangle of Mount Edith Cavell, shining above all others, to the south. The trail head is just across the river bridge on Old Fort Point Road.

**Head back to town, east (right) on Connaught Drive and north (left) on Pyramid Lake Road.**

**7 Pyramid and Patricia Lakes.** Head out in the early evening to spot wildlife on land (elk, deer, and moose) and in the water (beavers and ducks) just above town. Fishing is also a draw. Pyramid Island has a nice, short interpretive loop, great for watching the day come to an end.

# Yoho National Park

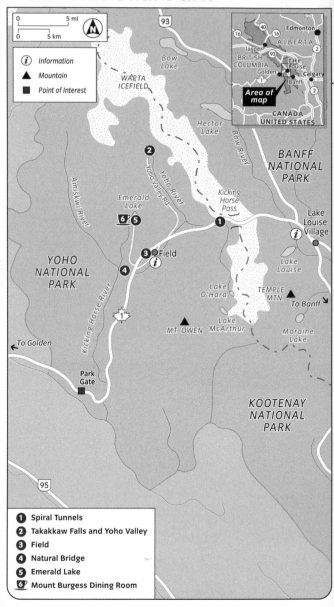

1 Spiral Tunnels
2 Takakkaw Falls and Yoho Valley
3 Field
4 Natural Bridge
5 Emerald Lake
6 Mount Burgess Dining Room

**Y**oho National Park makes a great base for exploring the
Rockies. You're midway between the Columbia Icefields and the
Town of Banff, next door to Lake Louise, and yet in a less traveled
area. "Yoho" is an expression of awe and wonder in the Cree language, and that's just what you'll experience in the park. This drive
takes you from Lake Louise southwest on the Trans-Canada Hwy. 1
through the park toward Golden, BC. START: **Lake Louise.**

Take the Trans-Canada Hwy. 1
west from Lake Louise 9.2km
(5¾ miles) to the border between
Alberta and British Columbia. Continue 8.7km (5½ miles) west of the
border and turn off into the roadside interpretive display at the:

❶ ★ **Spiral Tunnels.** The first
trains to make it over Kicking Horse
Pass had really difficult ascents going
toward Lake Louise, or wild rides
descending the steep west slope.
Engineers developed a groundbreak-
ing plan to ease the incline: the Spiral
Tunnels take trains through two
loops inside Cathedral Mountain,
easing the steepness substantially.
View the Spiral Tunnels from two
lookouts: The first (and best) is on
the side of Trans-Canada Hwy. 1 just
up the hill from Field and has excellent interpretive signs; the second is
on Yoho Valley Road just past the
Cathedral Mountain Bungalows.

Continue down the hill on the
Trans-Canada Highway another
3.7km (2⅓ miles), turning right at
Yoho Valley Road. Continue on to
the end.

❷ ★★ **Takakkaw Falls and the
Yoho Valley.** If you love waterfalls,
you've come to the right place:
"Takakkaw" means magnificent in
Cree. At 380m (1,247 ft.), this is the
fourth highest waterfall in Canada
and originates at the Daly Glacier
high above. There's a great picnic
spot at the base. Looking to the
north, you can often see the Yoho
Glacier on a clear day. This is also the
trail head for some superb hiking.

Drive back out to the Trans-Canada Hwy. 1, continuing 1.8km (1
mile) west to the turnoff for Field.

❸ ★ **Field.** This tiny town is the
service center for Yoho National
Park. It makes a good place to stop
for lunch but isn't worth a visit in
and of itself. Grab a sandwich, a coffee, and maybe pop into the pottery
shop and keep moving.

Turn left (west) on the Trans-Canada Highway and continue 2km
(1¼ miles) to the turnoff for Emerald Lake Road.

❹ **Natural Bridge.** Just south of
Field is the Natural Bridge, where the

*A freight train passes through the spiral tunnels of Kicking Horse Pass.*

# Lake O'Hara: Getting to Paradise

In Yoho National Park, the best hiking trails are at magical Lake O'Hara, a region that makes some locals misty-eyed just at its mention. There are some easy, shorter hikes around the lake itself, and a handful of excellent 3- to 6-hour trails that take you above Lake O'Hara to some of the equally spectacular surrounding lakes. The best bet is to connect all the short hikes into a challenging day hike known as the ★★★ **Lake O'Hara Circuit.**

Just on the other side of Lake Louise, O'Hara is accessed by a 13km (8-mile) road that can be hiked or cross-country skied in the winter. But daily Parks Canada–run bus rides (from mid-June to mid-Oct) will take you up to the warden station on the shores of Lake O'Hara in a painless 15 minutes. That'll give you the rest of the day for hiking. Reserve a spot on the bus by calling ☎ **250/343-6433.**

While you're on the line, you can also reserve a campsite at the Lake O'Hara Campground if you plan on staying the night at the lake. It's a good spot for families—it's in the backcountry, but accessible by bus so you don't have to worry about carrying everything in on your back.

Bus tickets cost $15 for adults and $7.30 for children, round-trip. Buses leave the parking lot daily at 8:30 and 10:30am. The last bus out departs the campground at 6:30pm.

The parking lot is located 1km (½ mile) west of the Alberta–British Columbia border, just off the south side of the Trans-Canada Hwy. 1. Turn south at the sign to Lake O'Hara and west into the parking lot. You must reserve campsites well in advance; the reservation line opens April 1. For more information, visit www.pc.gc.ca/yoho. Lake O'Hara Lodge has its own private bus service for its guests (see p 137).

*Hiking on the Lake O'Hara Alpine Circuit.*

Kicking Horse River meets with U-shaped sedimentary rock that has so far kept the river from breaking open a deep canyon. The river did manage to erode a small canyon of softer rock just upstream from the tougher section, creating a crooked bridge. Visit it soon—it may be gone in a matter of centuries! *Map p 106.*

**Drive 7km (4⅓ mile) until you reach:**

**5** ★★ **Emerald Lake.** Farther up the road from the Natural Bridge is the spectacular glacier-fed Emerald Lake, featuring hiking trails, canoe rentals, horse stables, and the lovely Emerald Lake Lodge (see p 137). A visit to Emerald Lake will fill you with wonder, and could fill an album worth of photos.

**6** **Mount Burgess Dining Room.** Finish the day on a high note. The seasonal fine dining inside this historic lodge is all about rustic Rocky Mountain cuisine with artistic flare.

*The Kicking Horse River passes underneath the Natural Bridge.*

The menu focuses on local game like elk, bison, and caribou, and there's an award-winning wine list with over 400 labels. *It's part of Emerald Lake Lodge. On Emerald Lake Rd., 8km (5 miles) off Trans-Canada Hwy. 1, at a turnoff 2km (1¼ miles) south of Field.* ☎ 250/343-6321. $$$.

# The Burgess Shale

The Rockies' greatest contribution to archaeology is the 515-million-year-old Burgess Shale, a fossil bed discovered at the base of Mount Stephen. This discovery transformed our understanding of the evolution of life on Earth and gave real examples of the amazing biodiversity that existed before the mass extinction of species—half of the animal groups seen in the shale have since disappeared from Earth. You can get there to see them only on a 6-hour, 6km (3¾-mile) guided hike organized by the Yoho Burgess Shale Foundation. This is a must for archaeology buffs, but you cannot drive to the Burgess Shale or visit it on your own; you must hike in to the site on an official tour with a registered guide. You will not enjoy this trip unless you are quite fit. Kids will enjoy the shorter hike to the Mount Stephen Fossil Beds.

Reserve in advance at www.burgess-shale.bc.ca or ☎ 800/343-3006 or 250/343-3006. Hike costs $100 adults, $50 students, $25 children under 12. It's available Friday through Monday from July 1 through Sept 15. The group takes only 15 fit hikers on one trip per day.

# Golden, British Columbia

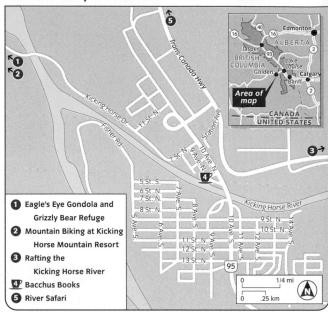

1. Eagle's Eye Gondola and Grizzly Bear Refuge
2. Mountain Biking at Kicking Horse Mountain Resort
3. Rafting the Kicking Horse River
4. Bacchus Books
5. River Safari

**G**olden is located just off the Trans-Canada Highway (Hwy. 1) at the confluence of the Kicking Horse and Columbia rivers. The small town has been on the verge of a boom for several years as it shifts gears from a resource-based economy to one based on outdoor recreation, largely due to the recently redeveloped Kicking Horse Mountain Resort. Although not located within Yoho National Park, Golden is the park's major gateway and service center. **START: Kicking Horse Mountain Resort is 14km (8⅔ miles) from Golden on Kicking Horse Trail Road.**

① ★★ **Eagle's Eye Gondola and Grizzly Bear Refuge.** Soar up to 2,350m (7,710 ft.) for a panoramic view of the Rocky and Purcell mountains. Hike the Terminator Ridge. Friday evenings and some Saturdays, the gorgeous restaurant opens for high altitude a la carte dining. Combine a gondola ride with a visit to the world's largest enclosed and protected grizzly bear refuge near the gondola's base. It's where Boo the grizzly lives and plays. *From Hwy. 95, turn west at blue sign for Kicking Horse Mountain Resort in downtown Golden, 13km/8 miles uphill.* ☎ *866/754-5425 or 250/439-5424. www.kickinghorse resort.com $31 adults, $28 ages 13–18 and seniors, $13 kids under 13. June 26–Sept 6 daily 10:30am–5:30pm; June 12–21 and Sept 11–27 Fri–Sun only.*

② **Mountain Biking.** When the snow leaves Kicking Horse Mountain Resort, the trails and the lifts are opened to two-wheelers for world-class downhill biking. Stick your bike

*A resident at the Grizzly Bear Refuge.*

on the gondola and cruise down twisty single-track trails. *At the base of Kicking Horse Mountain Resort.* ☎ *866/754-5425 or 250/439-5424; www.kickinghorseresort.com. Full-day bike ticket costs $36 for adults, youth, and seniors; $24 for kids 7–12. A one-time ticket with bike rental costs $60 for adults and $42 for kids 7–12.*

**From Kicking Horse Mountain Resort, head back into Golden. Drive through town and up the hill on Trans-Canada Hwy. 1. Twenty-five kilometers (16 miles) from Golden, turn right at the sign for Beaverfoot Lodge.**

❸ **White-Water Rafting.** The rapids on the Kicking Horse River are

some of the best in British Columbia. You'll dive through narrow canyons and see the valley from a totally different perspective. Plus, it's buckets of fun! Kootenay River Runners runs a half-day trip along the river. *1km/⅔ mile west of the western gates of Kootenay National Park.* ☎ *800/599-4399 or 250/347-9210; www.kootenayriver runners.com Rates are $90 with lunch. Children under 14 not permitted.*

**Back in Golden, turn right onto 6th Avenue and take a quick left onto 9th Street.**

❹ **Bacchus Books.** Sure, the eclectic first floor is chock-a-block with unique books, but follow your nose upstairs to the cafe and you'll discover fresh baked treats, natural and thick homemade soups, a roasted veggie Panini, or a smoked turkey wrap. *409 9th Ave. N.* ☎ *250/344-5600. www.bacchusbooks.com.* $

❺ **kids River Safari.** Jet-boat tours speed you through narrow canyons on the Columbia River. On-board naturalist guides will help you spot wildlife. *15km (9⅓ miles) west of Golden on Trans-Canada Hwy. 1. $90 adults, $70 kids 6–18.* ☎ *866/344-4931 or 250/344-4931. www.columbiariversafaris.ca.*

*White-water rafting on the Kicking Horse River.*

# Kootenay National Park

Hector Lake
Kicking Horse Pass
Bow River
Field
Lake Louise
Lake Louise Village
Lake Louise
Bow Valley Parkway
BANFF NATIONAL PARK
Lake O'Hara
TEMPLE MTN.
MT. OWEN
YOHO NATIONAL PARK
Moraine Lake
Castle Junction
CASTLE MTN.
CASCADE MTN.
Mt. Norquay
KOOTENAY NATIONAL PARK
Boom Lake
Redearth Creek
ISABELLE
Sunshine Village
Banff
Kootenay Parkway
Vermillion River
To Golden
Simpson River
BRITISH COLUMBIA
ALBERTA
Mt. Assiniboine Provincial Park
MT. ASSINIBOINE
Kootenay River
Edgewater
Park Gate
Radium Hot Springs

Area of map
Edmonton
ALBERTA
Jasper
BRITISH COLUMBIA
Golden
Lake Louise
Banff
Calgary
CANADA
UNITED STATES

**Legend**

- 🅰 Campground
- ⛽ Gasoline
- ✚ Hospital/First Aid
- ⓘ Information
- ▲ Mountain
- ■ Point of Interest
- 🎿 Ski Area

1. Fireweed Trail
2. Stanley Glacier
3. Marble Canyon
4. The Paint Pots
5. Kootenay Park Lodge
6. Kootenay Valley Lookout
7. Radium Hot Springs Pools
8. Sinclair Canyon

0        5 mi
0        5 km

A drive through **Kootenay National Park makes a great day trip** from Banff National Park. Established in 1920, the park is long and narrow (94km/58 miles long; 8km/5 miles across) and has a remarkably diverse landscape. The main road through the park traverses the scars of the massive 2003 forest fire; two large lighting-caused fires eventually merged and burned 12.6% of the park. It's a quiet park, with some interesting stops along the 94km (58-mile) Banff–Windermere Highway. It'll take you about 90 minutes to drive back from Radium Hot Springs directly to Banff. START: **Castle Junction, Banff National Park.**

Take Hwy. 93 west towards British Columbia.

**1** kids **Fireweed Trail.** Just past the Continental Divide and over the Alberta–British Columbia border, make a stop at the Vermillion Pass to hike the Fireweed Trail, a short 20-minute loop with interpretive signs that explain why natural forest fires are healthy and good for the environment and are no longer suppressed by Parks Canada. *On the south side of Hwy. 93, at the provincial border.*

Continue west on Hwy. 93.

**2** ★★ **Stanley Glacier.** Taking you from fire to ice in only 2.5km (1½ miles), this is a relatively short and only moderately steep half-day hike on the crest of the Continental

*Trees along the Fireweed Trail.*

*Water flowing through Marble Canyon.*

Divide. The family-friendly trail takes you up to a hanging valley with a giant glacier clinging to the limestone cliffs at the back. There are great views throughout the entire hike. Great in the morning. *On the south side of Hwy. 93, 3.2km (2 miles) past the provincial border.*

Continue west on Hwy. 93.

**3** ★★ **Marble Canyon.** If it's a hot day, you'll particularly enjoy a short hike at this narrow trail of limestone carved by two retreated glaciers. The farther up the trail you walk, the more impressive the canyon. It's cool and shady here. And

*Vintage cars parked outside the Kootenay Park Lodge.*

don't be fooled by the name: There is no marble, only white and gray dolomite rock. Kids will find the hike intriguing, but keep an eye on them because the trail can get slippery. *On the north side of Hwy. 93, 7km (4⅓ miles) past the provincial border.*

**Continue west on Hwy. 93.**

**4 The Paint Pots.** A brief and beautiful walk takes you to this fascinating area where First Nations people gathered ocher, an iron-based mineral that was baked, crushed, mixed with grease, and used as a paint for tepees, pictographs, and personal adornment. There is an excellent, wheelchair-friendly, 30-minute interpretive trail. *On the north side of Hwy. 93, 10km (6¼ miles) past the provincial border.*

**5 Kootenay Park Lodge.** The only place to stop and grab a bite to eat inside Kootenay National Park is at this historic lodge. Try the home-made burgers and "mountain fries." There's a Parks Canada–run information center next door with snacks, maps, and a friendly staff.

*Hwy. 93 at Vermillion Crossing, 42km (26 miles) west of Castle Junction, 61km (38 miles) east of Radium Hot Springs.* ☎ 403/762-9196.$$

**6 Kootenay Valley Lookout.** For an expansive lookout of the majestic 80-km (50-mile) Kootenay River Valley, pull off to the left or south-eastern side of Highway 93 at a wide turnoff just before the highway turns toward Sinclair Pass. You'll see the impact of the 2003 forest fires, as well as the diversity of the remaining forests to the south. Interpretive signs explain how the dramatic view has changed over time. *On southeast curve of Hwy 93 47 km (29 mi) south of Kootenay Park Lodge or 16 km (20 mi) north from Radium. Map p. 112.*

**Continue west on Hwy. 93.**

**7 ★ Radium Hot Springs Pools.** These "sacred mountain waters" have been drawing visitors to the Columbia Valley since 1914. There is one hot pool (104°F/40°C); and a cooler pool (81°F/27°C), both settled in a canyon rich with oxide,

# Radium

A small town (population 675) at the southern end of Kootenay National Park, Radium Hot Springs—often simply called Radium—is named for (you guessed it) its famous hot springs, which draw visitors to soak in their supposedly healing waters. The town is essentially a strip of motels and restaurants, but if you explore some of the back roads you'll discover a spectacular setting and bump into more than a few Calgary residents who make this their second home. It's also a good area for golfing and hiking—the Radium Resort (☎ 800/667-6444 or 250/347-6200; www.radium resort.com) has an 18-hole championship course located along the cliffs that border the Columbia River, or you can hike the Juniper Trail past Sinclair Canyon or the Valley View Trail which starts at Redstreak Campground.

giving the walls a permanent orange-sunset look. *3km (1¾ miles) northeast of the Town of Radium on Hwy. 93.* ☎ *250/347-9485. Admission $6.50 adults, $5.50 seniors and children. Mid-May to mid-Oct daily 9am–11pm; mid-Oct to mid-May Sun–Thurs noon–9pm, Fri–Sat noon–10pm.*

**Continue west on Hwy. 93.**

**8 Sinclair Canyon.** Kootenay closes with a bang at the spectacular red cliffs of Sinclair Canyon, which welcome you to the Columbia Valley just after the Radium Hot Springs pools.

*The popular Radium Hot Springs have been in business since 1914.*

# Calgary in One Day

**Legend**

- ℹ Information
- Ⓒ C-Train (Light rail)
- ⋯⋯ Walking/ Biking Path

1. Calgary Tower
2. Glenbow Museum
3. Stephen Avenue Mall
4. Art Gallery of Calgary
5. Olympic Plaza
6. Uptown 17th Ave.
7. Caffe Beano
8. Eau Clair Market
9. Prince's Island Park

**W**ith over a million people, a strong economy, and plenty of personality, Calgary is stepping boldly into its role as the "heart of the New West." Safe, clean, and young, Calgary has an identity that goes beyond white cowboy hats and rodeos. And while hipsters may snicker at the cowboy schtick, it is really authentic here. Western hospitality is legendarily friendly, upbeat, and relaxed. It's a fun and exciting city that is quite simple to discover. With a day or two, you can take in the main sites, and have a bit of time to wander in one of the city's top neighborhoods—Kensington or Inglewood stand out. START: **Calgary Tower.**

❶ ★★ **Calgary Tower.** Come here first to get your bearings 191m (627 ft.) in the sky. You can spot the Stampede Grounds and Pengrowth Saddledome (where the NHL's Calgary Flames play) to the southwest, the Bow River winding through town, and the snow-capped Rocky Mountains on the western horizon. *9th Ave. and Centre St.* ☎ *403/266-7171. www.calgarytower.com. Elevator ride $13 adults, $11 seniors, $9.95 youth 13–17, and $5 children 4–12. June–Aug daily 9am–10:30pm; Sept–May daily 9am–9:30pm.*

Walk one block east on 9th Ave. SE, turning left on 1st SE.

*The Calgary Tower, Memorial Drive, the Bow River, and the Calgary skyline.*

*A public art installation in the Stephen Avenue Mall.*

❷ **Glenbow Museum.** The walls and halls of this storied museum downtown tell the story of the West, from the past to the present. Start in the Blackfoot Gallery to learn about First Nations cultures; then continue on to the Mavericks Gallery, which celebrates today's groundbreakers. *130 9th Ave. SE, at 1st St.* ☎ *403/268-4100. www. glenbow.org. Admission $14 adults, $10 seniors, $9 students and youth. Fri–Wed 9am–5pm, Thurs 9am–9pm.*

*Olympic Plaza.*

**Turn left on 1st Street SE and left again at 8th Avenue SE, also known as Stephen Avenue.**

**③ Stephen Avenue Mall.** A pedestrian avenue that is lined by banks, high-end shops like Holt Renfrew and Birks, lively eateries, and some interesting public art, this is a great spot for lunch. Try **SaltLik** (101 8th Ave. SW; ☎ 403/537-1160) for steaks, the fashionable **Belvedere** (107 8th Ave. SW; ☎ 403/265-9595), or the chic **Blink** (111 8th Ave. SW; ☎ 403/263-5330).

**④ Art Gallery of Calgary.** Contemporary art's home in Calgary is in a historic building on convenient Stephen Avenue Mall. Evolving exhibits showcase a variety of media. Pop in for an hour at lunchtime for only $2. *117 8th Ave. SW,* ☎ *403/770-1350. www.artgallery calgary.org. $5 adults, $2.50 senior/youth, free children under 12. Tues–Sat 10am–5pm.*

**Walk past 1st Street SE to the far east end of Stephen Avenue.**

**⑤ Olympic Plaza.** A public square across the street from Calgary's stately, sandstone Old City Hall is at the eastern end of Stephen Avenue. Built for the medal ceremonies of the 1988 Winter Olympics,

this is where Calgarians come to celebrate everything from hockey victories to Reggaefest. In winter, there's an outdoor skating rink. *228 8th Ave. SE. ☎ 403/268-2489. Admission free.*

**From Stephen Avenue, turn left on 1st SWand walk 7 blocks south.**

**⑥ Uptown 17th Avenue.** Cross south and venture through a gentrifying neighborhood towards the eclectic, funky stretch of 17th Avenue. Fashion boutiques, vintage stores, clubs, coffee shops, and great bistros draw fashionistas, foodies, and those just looking for a nice stroll. *17th Ave. SW btw. 10th St. and 4th St. SW.*

**⑦ Caffe Beano.** At the corner of 17th Avenue and 9th Street, stop in here for a steaming latte. Espresso milkshakes will also pick you up. *1613 9 St. SW. ☎ 403/229-1232. $.*

**Hop in a cab or turn left at 4th Street SW and walk north 13 blocks, turning right on 2nd Avenue SW.**

**⑧ Eau Clair Market.** It's lacking some of its former freshness, but there is still lots of action happening around this complex on the edge of Calgary's downtown business core. Family-friendly pizza places, pubs, and nightclubs line the outside; specialty shops are inside. The food court is a good place for a cheap meal, and there's a movie theater upstairs. *200 Barclay Parade SW. www.eauclairemarket.com. Market building 9am–9pm, shops and restaurants have varied hours.*

**From behind the Market, pass the fountain and head on to the bridge over the Bow River.**

**❾ Prince's Island Park.** Where Calgarians come to stretch, run, bike, rollerblade, stroll, and play, this urban island can be beautiful on a warm spring or summer evening. A network of paths follows the Bow

*The patio at Prince's Island's River Café.*

River and connects with various arteries of the city. At the heart of the island is the outstanding River Café (see p 124). *Near 2nd Ave. SW and 3rd St. SW.*

## Calgary Stampede

If you're in Calgary during the first 2 weeks of July, well, yeehaw! The world-famous Calgary Stampede, calling itself the "Greatest Outdoor Show on Earth," takes over the city in a major way. It's the richest rodeo around, with $2 million in prizes. From morning stampede breakfasts and parades to a roller-coaster midway and live concerts, there is a lot to soak in. Visit www.calgarystampede.com for more information on the event and how to get tickets.

*Dishing out flapjacks at a Stampede breakfast.*

# Calgary in Two Days

1. Calgary Farmer's Market
2. Heritage Park
3. Calgary Olympic Park
4. Kensington

**Y**ou've seen all the main highlights of **Calgary** and its bustling downtown core. A second day will let you branch out to roam the wider regions of Calgary. But you'll need a vehicle for today's trip. START: **Calgary Farmer's Market, where you can grab a healthy breakfast.**

**①  Calgary Farmer's Market.** A year-round indoor market has rows and rows of seasonal produce, organic meat, and artwork from more than 100 vendors. *4421 Quesnay Wood Dr. SW.* ☎ *403/261-4548. Free admission. Thurs 11am–5pm; Fri–Sat 9am–5pm; Sun 9am–4pm.*

**Continue south on Crowchild Trail, turning east on Glenmore Trail. Turn south on 14th Street SW into the Glenmore Park.**

**②  Heritage Park.** A re-created pioneer village covers the years from 1860 to 1940. Ride on a steam train or paddlewheeler, or go for a ride on the antique midway. *1900 Heritage Dr. SW.* ☎ *403/268-8500. Adults $20, children 3–17 $15, families $70. May 16–Sept 7 daily 9am–5pm; rest of year Sat–Sun 9am–5pm.*

**Head north out of Glenmore Park onto 14th Street SW, turning west or left on Glenmore Trail. Follow until it meets up with the Trans-Canada Hwy. 1. Go west to the next exit.**

**③  Calgary Olympic Park.** The slopes which hosted luge, bobsleigh, and ski jumping in the 1988 Olympics has a small ski hill open to all during the winter. In summer, it turns into a playground with mountain biking, zip-lining, and great views from the top of the Ski Jump Tower. There's also an Olympic museum and Hall of Fame. *88 Canada Olympic Rd. SW.* ☎ *403/247-5452. Admission free; pay per activity. Hours vary.*

**Take the Trans-Canada Hwy. 1 east back towards the city. Turn east at Memorial Drive, following the Bow River until you reach Kensington Road.**

**④  Kensington.** To mix and mingle with Calgarians, head to Kensington Road. There are pubs, cafes, unique boutiques, some excellent restaurants—**Globefish**, on 14th Street just north of Kensington Road (☎ 403/521-0221) has the best sushi in Calgary—and a relaxed feel in one of the city's liveliest neighborhoods.

*The steam train travels through Heritage Park.*

# Calgary **Dining & Lodging**

**Accommodations**
Acclaim Hotel 11
The Fairmont Palliser 12
Holiday Inn Express 3
Hyatt Regency Calgary 14
Kensington
Riverside Inn 2
Sandman
Calgary West 1
Sheraton Suites 8

**Dining**
Avenue Diner 13
The Coup 5
Farm 4
Mercato 7
Peter's Drive In 10
The Ranche 6
River Café 9
Sky 360 15
Teatro 16

Information
C-Train (Light rail)
Walking/Biking Path

# Dining & Lodging A to Z

## Restaurants
### Avenue Diner DOWNTOWN
*DINER* For a hearty breakfast or lunch amidst the suit-and-tie crowd, grab a table in this narrow diner on the pedestrian Stephen Avenue Mall. It's mostly about breakfast and brunch. There's a variety of all-day "signature" eggs Benedicts to choose from, as well as comfort-food stars like meatloaf and macaroni and cheese. *105 8th Ave. ☎ 403/263-2673. Entrees $9–$16. AE, MC, V. Mon–Fri 7am–3pm; Sat–Sun 8am–3pm. Map p 122.*

### ★ The Coup 17th Avenue *VEGETARIAN* Healthy, fresh, creative fusion food stars at this hip spot on 17th Avenue. Most ingredients are vegetarian, organic, and local. There are jam-packed salads, falafel quesadillas, and a dragon bowl that has steamed veggies, tofu, and brown rice. There's also a fun cocktail list. *924 17th Ave. SW. ☎ 403/541-1041. Entrees $14–$22. AE, MC, V. Tues–Thurs 11:30am–3pm and 5–10pm; Fri 11:30am–3pm and 5–11pm; Sat 9am–3pm and 5–11pm; Sun 9am–3pm and 5–9pm.*

### ★ Farm 17th AVENUE *REGIONAL* Just as the name suggests, this a place to sample wholesome, simple food. It's classic "slow food" style, but it's more precious than most pastoral country tables. Small plates and platters make sampling from the outstanding cheese selection a good idea. The mac 'n' cheese is the best in town. The ambience is as relaxing as the countryside. *1006 17th Ave. SW. ☎ 403/245-2276. Entrees $8–$13. AE, MC, V. Daily 11:30am–10pm.*

### ★ Mercato MISSION *ITALIAN* Inside Calgary's swanky gourmet Italian deli, the restaurant is mainly counter-style. The simplified Italian food, however, is show-stealing, particularly the *bisteca fiorentina* rib-eye steak. It's an energetic, sometimes frantic place a few blocks from 17th Avenue in the upscale 4th Street–Mission district. *2224 4th St. SW. ☎ 403/263-5535. Entrees $12–$44. AE, MC, V. Daily 11:30am–2pm and 5–9pm. Map p 122.*

### kids Peter's Drive In NORTH OF DOWNTOWN *DINER* If you're en route to Banff from the Calgary airport (or vice versa), drop by this legendary and truly retro (it's been around since 1964) "drive-in" for burgers, fries, onion rings, and a shake. You can be served in the car or go through the drive-through window. It's right on the Trans-Canada Hwy. 1. *219 16th Ave. ☎ 403/277-2747. Entrees $8–$14. No credit cards. Daily 9am–midnight. Map p 122.*

*The open-concept kitchen at Farm.*

★ **The Ranche** SOUTH OF DOWN-TOWN *REGIONAL*   Whisk yourself out into the country, only 20 minutes from downtown at this lovely restaurant inside a heritage ranch home in Fish Creek Provincial Park. As expected, there's a lot of meat and game, usually offered in tandem with gentle details, like a bison rib-eye with wild mushroom ragout and mustard spaetzle. Also great for a weekend brunch. *In Fish Creek Park, off Bow Bottom Trail.* ☎ *403/225-3939. Entrees $24–$38. AE, MC, V. Mon–Thurs 11:30am–2pm and 5–9pm; Fri 11:30am–2pm and 5–10pm; Sat 5–10pm; Sun 10:30am–2pm and 5–9pm. Map p 122.*

★★ **River Café** PRINCE'S ISLAND PARK *REGIONAL*   From the picturesque setting in a wooden lodge on an island in the Bow River to a menu that exemplifies regional and seasonal Alberta cuisine, this is a rich experience. Start with the emblematic fish and game platter. Then opt for bison or beef. If you're only in town for 1 night and it's not storming out, then this should be your choice for dinner. *Prince's Island Park.* ☎ *403/261-7670. Entrees $27–$49. AE, MC, V. Mon–Fri 11am–3pm; Sat–Sun 10am–3pm and daily 5–11pm. Map p 122.*

★★ **Sky 360** DOWNTOWN *REGIONAL*   There's more than just spectacular views 762 steps up from the ground in the Calgary Tower. The menu is now much more gourmet-focused and upscale, but is also full of crowd-pleasers like goat cheese penne, grilled salmon, tenderloins, and striploins. The elevator fee is included, the wine list excellent, and with the place rotating on a 45-minute schedule, you'll get a couple of full city views and time to relax. *In the Calgary Tower. 101 9th Ave. SW.* ☎ *403/532-7966. Entrees $21–$45. AE, MC, V. Mon–Sat 11am–2pm and 5–9pm. Sun 9:30am–2pm and 5–9pm. Map p 122.*

★★ **Teatro** DOWNTOWN *EUROPEAN*   For a refined, romantic meal, come to this dazzling room inside the historic Dominion Bank building. It's mainly Italian food, since the owner is Italian, but there's a delicate high-end French influence. Pastas come with duck Bolognese or Atlantic lobster sauces, for example. Drop in for a martini or a glass of wine before going to a show, or for a nightcap. *200 8th Ave. SE, Olympic Plaza.* ☎ *403/290-1012. Entrees $26–$49. AE, DC, MC, V. Mon–Fri 11:30am–10pm; Sat and Sun 5–10pm. Map p 122.*

## Accommodations

**Acclaim Hotel** AIRPORT   If all you need is a good bed before or after your flight, this new airport hotel is a great choice. Complimentary shuttle, big fluffy beds, a rooftop hot tub, and a fitness club will ease your travel-weary bones. It's way out of town, though. *123 Freeport Blvd. NE.* ☎ *866/955-0008 or 403/291-8000. www.acclaimhotel.ca. 123 units. Doubles $144–$154. AE, MC, V. Map p 122.*

*Teatro is located inside the historic Dominion Bank building.*

★ **The Fairmont Palliser** DOWN-TOWN   Opened in 1914, this historic landmark has deep roots in the Calgary community. Rooms here are notoriously cramped, as in most urban hotels of this vintage, but they retain an old-world elegance typical of Fairmont. The new Fairmont Gold rooms have extra value with a private concierge, private check-in, and separate dining area. The lobby could use some freshening up. *133 9th Ave. SW.* ☎ *800/441-1414 or 403/262-1234. www.fairmont.com. 405 units. Doubles $149–$449. AE, DC, DISC, MC, V. Map p 122.*

**kids** **Holiday Inn Express** DOWNTOWN   My choice for best mid-range hotel in town, this includes the predictable high-rise hotel experience found in many hotels, plus breakfast. The rooms are average and the location good. There's a small fitness center. Kids eat free in the grill next door. *1020 8th Ave.* ☎ *877/660-8550 or 403/269-4868. www.hiexpress.com. 56 units. Doubles $189–$225. AE, MC, DC, V. Map p 122.*

**Hyatt Regency Calgary** DOWNTOWN   Of all the chains downtown, this is probably the best. That's because it's the newest and because it's stylishly tucked right into the facade of the historic Stephen Avenue Mall. Rooms are very large. The amazing Stillwater Spa is worth checking out. *700 Centre St.* ☎ *800/233-1234 or 403/717-1234. www.calgary.hyatt.com. 355 units. Doubles $152–$269. AE, MC, DC, V. Map p 122.*

★★ **Kensington Riverside Inn** KENSINGTON   With more flair and personality than just about every other hotel in town, this boutique inn—on the north side of the river a short walk from downtown—is private, expensive, design-forward,

*The dining area at the Hyatt Regency Calgary.*

and chic. The rooms are large, the ambiance cool, and the new restaurant possibly the hottest in town. *1126 Memorial Dr. NW.* ☎ *877/313-3733. www.kensingtonriversideinn.com. 19 units. Doubles $289–$359. AE, DC, MC, V. Map p 122.*

**Sandman Calgary West** WEST OF DOWNTOWN   Across the road from Canada Olympic Park, this is the last hotel in town before you hit the road to Banff. It's entirely functional, with an indoor pool and a 24-hour restaurant. If you want a place to crash before hitting the road or if you want to beat traffic in or out of town, this is a good bet. It's 20 minutes from downtown. *125 Bowridge Dr.* ☎ *800/726-3626 or 403/288-6033. www.sandmanhotels.com. 121 units. Doubles $143–$197. AE, MC, V. Map p 122.*

**Sheraton Suites** DOWNTOWN   Overlooking the Bow River and Eau Claire Market, the location here is very convenient. Since all the rooms are suites, there's a sense of luxury and efficiency that'll appeal to larger families or business travelers. *255 Barclay Parade.* ☎ *888/784-8370 or 403/266-7200. www.sheratonsuites.com. 323 suites. Suites $169–$289. AE, DC, MC, V. Map p 122.*

# Alberta Rockies **Dining & Lodging**

**Jasper**

Dining
Andy's Bistro **7**
Bears Paw Bakery **3**
Earl's **2**
Fiddle River **10**
Jasper Brewing
  Company **11**
Moose's Nook
  Northern Grill **5**
North Face Pizza **9**
Palisades **4**

Lodging
Alpine Village **13**
Coast Pyramid
  Lake Resort **1**
Fairmont Jasper
  Park Lodge **6**
Jasper International
  Hostel **14**
Mount Edith Cavell Hostel **17**
Park Place Inn **8**
Pine Bungalows **12**
Wapiti Campground **16**
Whistlers Campground **15**

Pyramid Lake Rd
Elm
Hazel Ave
Gelkie
Patricia
Connaught Dr
Athabasca River
16
93A
Miette River
93
To Banff

△ Campground
✚ Hospital/First Aid
P Parking

0 — 1/4 mi
0 — .25 km

**Canmore**

0 — 1/4 mi
0 — .25 km

17th St.
7th Ave.
1st Ave.
1A
15th St.
14th St.
8th Ave.
Fairholme Dr.
13th St.
11th St.
River Rd.
Bow River
10th St.
9th St.
7th Ave.
8th St.
Main St.
P
7th St.
6th St.
8th Ave.
7th Ave.
5th St.
4th St.
Railway Ave.
Old Bridge
Trans-Canada Highway
Hospital Pl.
Policman's Creek
Benchlands Trail
Kananaskis Way
Montane Rd.
1A
1

✚ Hospital
P Parking
••• Walking Path

Dining
Communitea Café **3**
Crazyweed Kitchen **4**
Rocky Mountain
  Flatbread Company **5**
The Trough Dining Company **1**

Lodging
Blackstone Mountain
  Lodge **7**
Delta Lodge at Kananaskis **8**
Paintbox Lodge **6**
Rocky Mountain Ski Lodge **2**

Bear's Paw Bakery.

but classy wine list. *606 Patricia St.* ☎ *780/852-4559. Reservations recommended. Entrees $22–36. AE, MC, V. Mon–Sat 5–11pm. Map p 126.*

**Bear's Paw Bakery** JASPER *BAKERY/CAFE* With two locations, this bakery is very popular. There are fresh sandwiches, granola to go, superb fruit tarts, and a huge variety of cookies, bars, and yummy delights—including dog treats. Their freshly baked bread is served at nearly every restaurant in town. *610 Connaught Dr. and 4 Cedar Ave.* ☎ *780/852-3233. Sandwiches $7–$12. AE, MC, V. Daily 7am–6pm. Map p 126.*

★★ **Communitea Café** CANMORE *CAFE/VEGETARIAN* Choose from more than 80 blends of loose-leaf tea at this funky hangout. Lunches are healthy, affordable, and tasty. Build your own rice bowl with organic brown rice, steamed veggies, and flavorful Asian sauces. There are also great snacks like sushi, shrimp rolls, organic edamame—and quite possibly the best lattes in town, brewed in a one-of-a-kind espresso machine. This is a place with heart. *117–1001*

## Restaurants

★ **Andy's Bistro** JASPER *EUROPEAN* It's the consistency, with great-quality food and good service, that keeps this as a top choice in Jasper. The best dishes are traditional Swiss blended with tastes from around the world, like veal emince Zurich-style and filet mignon with pesto and goat cheese. Portions are very large. There's a casual

*The chaotic Crazyweed Kitchen.*

6th Ave., corner of 10th St. ☎ 403/
678-6818. Entrees $8–$14. MC, V.
Mon–Sat 9am–5pm; Sun 10am–5pm.
Map p 126.

★ **Crazyweed Kitchen** CANMORE
GLOBAL/FUSION  Slightly unpre-
dictable and always provocative,
the Crazyweed's new location is
both chaotic and creative. The food
here could just be the most incredible of your life, particularly the kash-
miri lamb balls and the Thai grilled
chicken. But service is erratic, either
pompously absent or delightfully
charming. 1600 Railway Ave. ☎ 403/
609-2530. Entrees $24–$38. AE, MC,
V. Sat and Sun 10:30am–3pm; Mon–
Fri 11:30am–3pm; daily 5–10pm.
Map p 126.

**Earl's** JASPER CANADIAN  A real
crowd-pleaser, Earl's is a good choice
for just about anybody—families, cou-
ples, or friends. Part of a popular
Western Canada chain, there's a bit of
Mexican, Asian, and European served
here, from burgers to Thai curries to
brick-oven pizzas. They also have the
nicest outdoor patio in town, including heaters on a chilly evening. 600
Patricia St., upstairs. ☎ 780/852-
2393. Reservations recommended in
summer. Entrees $12–$32. AE, MC, V.
Daily 11:30am–midnight. Map p 126.

**Fiddle River** JASPER CANADIAN
Upstairs, above Connaught Street,
there's an ever-changing menu here
that almost always has Canadiana
favorites like Alberta-raised beef,
caribou meatloaf, and a steaming
bison stew, as well as pumpkin-seed
trout and a seafood kettle. The service is casual and friendly, and the
views are divine. 620 Connaught St.,
upstairs. ☎ 780/852-3032. Entrees
$18–$35. AE, MC, V. Daily 5pm–midnight. Map p 126.

**Jasper Brewing Company** JAS-
PER BREWPUB  A warm and cozy
place for a pint and a burger, the
bartender will suggest the fish and
chips or sirloin steak burger. There
are big-screen TVs and a cozy fireplace. Highly regarded ales, pil-
sners, and stouts are brewed in the
back; a sample of six costs $13. 624
Connaught Dr. ☎ 780/852-4111.
Entrees $11–$26. AE, MC, V. Daily
11:30am–1am. Map p 126.

★★ **Moose's Nook Northern
Grill** JASPER REGIONAL  The best
meal in Jasper is to be had at the
Jasper Park Lodge's second-tier
restaurant (after the white-glove
Edith Cavell Dining Room). With
unforgettable meals like boar
bacon–wrapped bison tenderloin,

A dish from the highly regarded Moose's Nook Northern Grill inside the Jasper Park
Lodge.

*A kid-sized flatbread pizza from the Rocky Mountain Flatbread Company.*

great service, and live jazz most nights, the only thing lacking is a good view. *In the Fairmont Jasper Park Lodge, Old Lodge Rd.* ☎ 780/852-6052. *Entrees $28–$39, AE, DC, MC, V. Daily 6pm–9pm. Map p 126.*

**North Face Pizza** JASPER *PIZZA* If you want to order in, do so from Jasper's best pizza joint. Free delivery anywhere in town. There are also burgers, salads, pastas, sandwiches, and wings on offer, plus locally brewed beer from Big Rock Brewery on tap. Eat in (order at the counter) if you want to mingle with the local under-30 crowd. *618 Connaught Dr.* ☎ 780/852-5830. *Pizzas $12–$26. AE, MC, V. Daily 11am–2am. Map p 126.*

**Palisades** JASPER *GREEK/CANADIAN* Jasper has a surprisingly strong Greek community and many restaurants offer souvlaki, paithaika, and moussaka. Palisades, however, has the best. The food is simple and good, and the prices great. *401 Patricia St., at the corner of Cedar.* ☎ 780/852-5222. *Entrees $8–$21. MC, V. Daily 3–11pm. Map p 126.*

**kids Rocky Mountain Flatbread Company** CANMORE *MEDITERRANEAN* The wood-fired clay oven here is allegedly the largest in Canada. Handcrafted flatbread pizzas are made with organic flour, regional cheeses, and fresh, creative toppings. The Nemo has prawns, artichokes, and asiago cheese. Pint-sized portions for kids and a kid-friendly play area, where they can bake their own pretend pizzas, are available. *838 10th St.* ☎ 403/609-5508. *Entrees $14–$28. AE, MC, V. July–Aug daily 11:30am–10pm; Sept–June daily 5–10pm. Map p 126.*

**★★★ The Trough Dining Co.** CANMORE *BISTRO* With a relaxed and intimate vibe, this is Canmore's top restaurant. Flavors are powerful and intense in every dish. Labor-intensive entrees include organic chicken tikka and jerk-spiced baby back pork ribs, both chock full of fresh ingredients and surprising tastes. Staff is highly professional and the wine list extensive. If you're on a budget, come for a glass of wine and dessert. *725 9th St., behind Main St. btw. 6th and 7th aves.* ☎ 403/678-2820. *Reservations highly recommended. Entrees $26–$35. AE, MC, V. Sun, Mon, Wed, and Thurs 6–10pm; Fri and Sat 5–11pm. Map p 126.*

**Accommodations**

**★★ Alpine Village** JASPER On the banks of the rushing Athabasca River, these rustic yet stylish log cottages make a cozy, romantic base, good for simply enjoying the natural beauty of the park. They range from brand-new deluxe bedroom suites to quaint cabins dating back to 1941. All have some form of a kitchenette. Cabins farthest from the road are quieter, but those along the river (next to the road) have the best views. *2.5km (1½ miles) south of Jasper Townsite on*

*One of the rustic cottages at Alpine Village.*

the Icefields Pkwy., Hwy. 93, at the junction with Hwy. 93A. ☎ 780/852-3285. www.alpinevillagejasper.com. 41 units, 28 with kitchenettes. Cabins $180–$360. MC, V. Closed mid-Oct to end of April. Map p 126.

### Blackstone Mountain Lodge

CANMORE   Settle into your own condo at this new vacation rental property. The decor is urban chic, but the views are definitely all natural. Fully equipped units have one, two, or three bedrooms, private balconies, granite countertops, stainless steel appliances, and even a wine cabinet. A good base if you're coming for a week or more. *170 Kananaskis Way.* ☎ *888/830-8883 or 403/609-8098. www.blackstone canmore.ca. 123 units. Weekly rates $835–$1,339. AE, MC, V. Map p 126.*

### Coast Pyramid Lake Resort

JASPER   With a picturesque lakeside setting, this small resort offers plenty of activities, solitude, and lovely new rooms. Walls are thin. The top-floor Cavell Rooms, built in the late 1990s, are the largest and most modern guest rooms, perfect for families planning on staying a few days. It's slow-paced up here and you'll need a car. *6km (3¾ miles) north from Jasper Townsite on Pyramid Lake Rd.* ☎ *800/663-1144 or 780/852-4900. www.coasthotels. com. 62 units. Doubles $249–$299. AE, DC, MC, V. Map p 126.*

### Delta Lodge at Kananaskis

KANANASKIS COUNTRY   The premier hotel in "K-Country" sits at the heart of the multi-sport village, with a shopping arcade, restaurants, and trails at your doorstep. It's a big place and typically hosts conferences (it hosted the G8 Leaders Summit in 2002). The Signature Club

*The urban décor at Blackstone Mountain Lodge.*

*A public area inside the historic Fairmont Jasper Park Lodge.*

rooms are more private and include breakfast. Great spot for golfers. *1 Centennial Dr., Kananaskis Village.* ☎ *800/268-1111 or 403/591-7711. www.deltalodgeatkananaskis.ca. 321 units. Doubles $269–$359. AE, DC, MC, V. Map p 126.*

### ★★★ Fairmont Jasper Park Lodge

Built in 1923, this historic lodge epitomizes the pampered wilderness experience. It's like an upscale summer camp for adults spread over the largest commercial property in the Canadian Rockies (with a revered golf course, gorgeous lake, stables, and outdoor pool). The guest rooms are mostly in single-story cabins and cottages spread throughout the property. Ask about packages and promotions. *4km (2½ miles) east of Jasper on Hwy. 16, 3.2km (2 miles) southeast off Maligne Lake Rd.* ☎ *800/441-1414 or 780/852-3301. Fax 780/852-5107. www.fairmont.com/jasper. 446 units. Doubles $199–$599. AE, DC, DISC, MC, V. Map p 126.*

### Jasper International Hostel

JASPER   This is the best choice for budget travelers in Jasper, but it's best if you have a car. There are two dorms that are very big, where you'll sleep in bunk beds. Bathrooms are all shared. Family rooms are also available. The shared kitchen is very handy. There is a fun full-time activity program that will get you out exploring Jasper. *4km (2½ miles) south of Jasper Townsite on Hwy. 93, turn west on Tramway Rd. and follow for 3km (1¾ miles).* ☎ *877/852-0781 or 780/852-3215. www.hihostels.ca. 5 units (2 dormitory-style rooms and 3 private family rooms), 84 beds total. Doubles $63–$71. MC, V. Map p 126.*

### Mount Edith Cavell Hostel

JASPER   This simple shelter is a good base for backpackers and hikers. It sleeps 32 people in two cabins. It also has no electricity or flush toilets, but there's a self-catering kitchen and awe-inspiring scenery all around. Private doubles are available. Members of Hostelling International receive a discount. Open mid-June to mid-October only. *On Cavell Rd.; take Hwy. 93A south from the townsite to Cavell Rd.; turn west and continue for 13km/8 miles to the hostel, on the east side of the road.* ☎ *866/762-4122 or 780/852-3215. www.hihostels.ca. 32 beds. Doubles $60–$68. MC, V. Map p 126.*

### ★★ Paintbox Lodge

CANMORE   A winner for its cozy vibe, friendly service, and location (just steps from Main St.), this is Canmore's best boutique-style inn. The eight

*The cozy Paintbox Lodge.*

**★★ Park Place Inn** JASPER    This is the only place in town one could call an upscale boutique inn, with reasonable rates to boot. The 12 spacious rooms have a cowboy heritage theme, with beautiful linens, goose-down duvets, hardwood floors, huge tubs (many are claw-foot style), and plenty of space. Located upstairs on the bustling Patricia Street, it feels downtown (if that's possible in Jasper). *623 Patricia St.* ☎ *866/852-9770 or 780/852-9770. www.parkplaceinn.com. 14 rooms. Doubles $229–$269. AE, MC, V. Map p 126.*

guest rooms are all different and all comfortable; upstairs ones have high ceilings with a cozy sitting area. The two-bedroom suite is good for families. Service is hands-off and low-key, so be prepared to fend for yourself. *629 10th St.* ☎ *888/678-6100 or 403/609-0482. www.paintboxlodge.com. 8 units. Doubles $199–$279 AE, MC, V. Map p 126.*

**Pine Bungalows** JASPER    Cabins ensconced along the Athabasca River are nostalgic and family-friendly. Most of them have fireplaces, and nearly all of them have kitchenettes. The best cabins are nos. 1 through 12, right on the river. A good choice if you don't need to be pampered and want your privacy. *Just off Hwy. 16 and the Jasper Townsite turnoff.* ☎ *780/852-3491. www.pinebungalows.com. 72 cabins, 57 with kitchens and 25 motel*

*Canmore's Rocky Mountain Ski Lodge is reasonably priced and dependable.*

*A tent site at Whistlers Campground.*

rooms. Cabins $155–$210. AE, MC, V. Map p 126.

### Rocky Mountain Ski Lodge

CANMORE   A locally-owned classic in Canmore, rooms here are reasonably priced if basic, but it's been around for a long time and service is extremely dependable. Kids can roam about the parkland. It's good for budget ski trips. Ask for a room at the back of the property. *1711 Bow Valley Trail.* ☎ *800/665-6111 or 403/678-5445. www.rockyski.ca. 83 units. Doubles $119–$149. AE, MC, V. Map p 126.*

### Wapiti Campground JASPER

This is the only campground in the park that's open year-round, and in summer its quieter than Whistler's. There are 362 sites, 322 of which are for tents only. More than a third of the sites remain accessible in winter. There are often elk roaming about here—remember to keep your distance. *4km (2½ miles) south of Jasper Townsite on the Icefields Pkwy., Hwy. 93, on the east side.*

*Summer: 362 sites, 40 with electrical hookup. $27 tents; $32 RVs. Open Victoria Day long weekend (late May) and mid-June to early Sept. Winter: 93 sites, 40 with electrical hookup. $18 tents; $22 RVs. Open early Oct to early May. Map p 126.*

### Whistlers Campground JASPER

This is the biggest campground in Jasper, with 781 sites. It's also just south of town, on the Icefields Parkway (Hwy. 93). It can feel busy and noisy. There are fun interpretive programs put on in the summer evenings. Of the 177 RV sites, 100 have electrical hookups only; the other 77 sites have full hookups. I've twice seen a bear here—so keep your food stored properly. *3km (1¾ miles) south of Jasper Townsite on the Icefields Pkwy., Hwy. 93, on the west side. 781 sites, 100 with electrical hookup only, 77 with full hookup. $23–$27 tents; $32 electrical hookup; $38 full hookup. Open early May to early Oct. Map p 126.*

# BC Rockies **Dining & Lodging**

**Dining**

Cedar House Restaurant **8**
Horsethief Creek Pub **11**
Jita's Café **7**
Meet on Higher Ground
  Coffee House **10**
Truffle Pigs Bistro **4**

**Lodging**

Bighorn Meadows Lodge **9**
Cathedral Mountain Lodge **3**
Copper Horse Lodge **6**
Emerald Lake Lodge **2**
Lake O'Hara Lodge **5**
Radium Resort **13**
Redstreak Campground **12**
Twin Falls Chalet **1**

# Dining & Lodging A to Z

## Restaurants

### ★★ Cedar House Restaurant

GOLDEN *CANADIAN* Fresh and inspired food in a rural setting, the passionate chefs here offer simple and local ingredients, creating entrees like roasted free-range chicken supreme, slow-braised lamb shank, and a spectacular pan-seared peppered duck breast. Meats are all natural, and the fish is wild. For dessert, there are homemade sorbets. *735 Hefti Rd.* ☎ *250/344-4679. Entrees $15–$38. MC, V. Daily 5pm-9pm. Map p 134.*

### Horsethief Creek Pub RADIUM

*PUB* The menu here is almost as expansive as the views across the Columbia Valley. The famous half-pound burger comes with mushrooms, bacon, and melted cheese. Pasta lovers will be tempted by Kootenai curry fettuccini or Louisiana prawn penne. It's also a nice spot for an afternoon beer and nibbles. *7538 Main St.* ☎ *250/347-6400. Entrees $12–$26. MC, V. Sun–Thurs 11am–10pm; Sat–Sun 11am–11pm.*

Pub open weekends until midnight. *Map p 134.*

### Jita's Café GOLDEN *CAFE* For a

healthy meal or a mid-afternoon coffee break, head to this funky cafe in downtown Golden. Besides baked goods that are served fresh out of the oven, there are soups, sandwiches, and salads. I particularly like the Thai Asian salad. *B–1007 11th St.* ☎ *250/344-3660. Sandwiches $6–$12. No credit cards. Mon–Sat 8am–6pm; Sun 10am–4pm. Map p 134.*

### Meet on Higher Ground Coffee House RADIUM *CAFE* The

options in Radium aren't great, but this cozy cafe has by far the best coffee and baked goods in the village. Breakfast bagels and hearty sandwiches make for good picnics. *7527 Main St., Ste 6.* ☎ *250/347-6567. Breakfasts and sandwiches $5–$12. MC, V. Daily 6am–5pm. Map p 134.*

### ★★ Truffle Pigs Bistro FIELD

*CAFE* Field took center stage for foodies when this cafe became a

*A burger from the Horsethief Creek Pub.*

*Field's Truffle Pigs Bistro.*

bistro and moved across the street. The chef offers options like coconut curry ragout and an unforgettable lamb and fig sandwich. Handmade desserts and a good wine list make it the best stop between Lake Louise and Golden. *100 Centre St.* ☎ *250/343-6303. Lunch $9–$21; dinner entrees $14–$36. MC, V. Daily 9am–9pm. Map p 134.*

### Accommodations
### Bighorn Meadows Lodge

RADIUM    At last something besides a motel in Radium. These are

*Cathedral Mountain Lodge's "Grand Room."*

vacation rentals at a new condo development on the west side of town. They're new, so they're clean and have great views. Units have private balconies with barbecues overlooking the golf course. Guest rooms are a bargain but don't have kitchens. *10 Bighorn Blvd., Radium Hot Springs, BC.* ☎ *877/344-2323 or 250/347-2323. www.bighorn meadows.ca. 96 units. Apartments $139–$418. AE, MC, V. Map p 134.*

### ★★ Cathedral Mountain Lodge

FIELD    If it's a cozy log cabin in a peaceful and powerful setting you're after, this is an excellent choice. This lodge offers a beautiful blend of privacy and luxury tucked beneath its namesake mountain along the banks of the glacier-fed Kicking Horse River. Quintessential cabins are functional and cute, with fireplaces, modern bathtubs, and fluffy duvets. *Take the Trans-Canada Hwy. 5km (3 miles) west from the Alberta–British Columbia border or 2km (1¼ miles) east of Field, BC and turn northwest on Yoho Valley Rd.; continue 4km (2½ miles) to lodge.* ☎ *866/619-6442 or 250/343-6442. www.cathedralmountainlodge. com. 31 units. Cabins $195–$500. AE, MC, V. Map p 134.*

### Copper Horse Lodge GOLDEN

At the base of Kicking Horse Mountain Resort, this boutique-sized inn has a stylish mountain vibe, lovely service, and a supremely relaxing feel. Built only a few years ago, it's a good choice if your aim is to rip it up at the resort or find some quiet romance. Otherwise, it's out of the way. *At end of Kicking Horse Mtn. Rd.; turn right after the gondolas.* ☎ *877/544-7644 or 250/344-7644. www.copperhorselodge.com. 10 units. Doubles $180–$230. MC, V. Map p 134.*

★ **Emerald Lake Lodge** This luxurious but cozy lodge, made up of 24 buildings on 5 hectares (12 acres) in the heart of Yoho National Park is splendid. Each guest room has a fieldstone fireplace and warm, rustic decor, including dark green marble vanities in many bathrooms (although others remain in need of a facelift). Most rooms have a balcony. The real star, however, is Emerald Lake itself, a glow of turquoise that never escapes the corner of your eye. *Take Trans-Canada Hwy. 2km (1¼ miles) south of Field to Emerald Lake Rd. turnoff; continue 8km (5 miles).* ☎ *800/663-6336 or 250/343-6321. www.crmr.com. 85 units. Doubles $188–$455. AE, MC, V. Map p 134.*

*A room inside the Emerald Lake Lodge.*

★★★ **Lake O'Hara Lodge** YOHO NATIONAL PARK In a secluded alpine valley, there are no phones, no television, no roads, and no cars here (see the box "Lake O'Hare: Getting to Paradise," p 108). This is a paradise that is one of a kind. Cabins have comfortable beds and modern bathrooms; meals are included. It's a wonderful getaway for city slickers and a true mecca for mountain lovers of all ages. Reserve well in advance. *Access via the Parks*

*A room inside the Copper Horse Lodge.*

*One of the cabins at Lake O'Hara Lodge.*

*Canada bus that leaves the Lake O'Hara parking lot.* ☎ *250/343-6418. June–Sept and Oct–May* ☎ *403/678-4110. www.lakeohara.com. 8 lodge rooms, 8 cabins. Rates include all meals, tips, taxes, and bus transportation. Doubles $485–$678. No credit cards. Map p 134.*

**Radium Resort** RADIUM HOT SPRINGS   This relaxed four-season resort is primarily for golfers. Accommodations are moderately priced. The rooms are all large, and most have excellent views and large balconies. The two-level lofts are great for families and groups. *4km (2½ miles) south of Radium on Hwy. 93/95, east side.* ☎ *800/667-6444 or 250/347-9311. Fax 250/347-6299. www.radiumresort.com. 90 units. Doubles $109–$189. AE, MC, V. Map p 134.*

**Redstreak Campground** RADIUM HOT SPRINGS   There's lots to do at Parks Canada's largest campground in Kootenay National Park, including

nightly entertainment in the summer and a network of trails heading into the park. It's located behind the Visitors Centre. Reserve a campsite online at www.pccamping.ca or call ☎ 877/737-3783. *2.5km (1½ miles) southwest of Radium Hot Springs, turn east off Hwy. 93 at the sign.* ☎ *250/ 347-9505. 242 sites, 38 with electrical hookup only, 50 with full hookup. $27– $38. AE, MC, V. Open May 11–Oct 8. Map p 134.*

**Twin Falls Chalet** YOHO NATIONAL PARK   Tucked beneath one of the loveliest waterfalls in Yoho (and the competition is fierce!), this historic log cabin was built in 1908 and offers simple, rustic backcountry lodging for hikers. There is no electricity, although solar panels keep things warm and bright. *In Yoho Valley. Reserve by telephone only at* ☎ *403/228-7079. 15 beds. $250 per person, 2-night minimum, includes all meals. No credit cards. Open late June to mid-Sept. Map p 134.* ●

# 6 The Great Outdoors

# The Best **Hiking in Banff**

Campground
Gasoline
Hospital/First Aid
Information
Mountain
Point of Interest
Ski Area

Edmonton

ALBERTA

Lake
Louise

Calgary

Banff

Jasper

BRITISH
COLUMBIA

Golden

CANADA
UNITED STATES

Area of
map

BANFF
NATIONAL
PARK

Red Deer River

Siffleur
Wilderness

Bow River

Hector
Lake

Icefields Parkway

Peyto
Lake

WAPTA
ICEFIELD

Park
Gate

Saskatchewan
Crossing

Saskatchewan
RIVER

Saskatchewan
River

FRESHFIELD ICEFIELD

LYELL
ICEFIELD

To Jasper National Park

COLUMBIA
ICEFIELD

*Previous Page: Canoeing on Upper Waterfowl Lake.*

1. Cascade Ampitheatre
2. C-Level Cirque
3. Sundance Canyon
4. Castle Lookout
5. Cory Pass
6. Ink Pots
7. Sunshine Meadows
8. Lake Agnes/Beehives
9. Lakeshore Trail
10. Moraine Lakeshore Trail
11. Paradise Valley/Larch Valley
12. Plain of the Six Glaciers
13. Saddleback Pass
14. Bow Glacier Falls
15. Helen Lake
16. Nigel Pass
17. Parker Ridge
18. Peyto Lake/Bow Summit
19. Wilcox Pass

**T**he hiking season in Banff usually gets started in early June and winds down in October. Trails on the southern slopes and at lower elevations are free of snow earlier in the season and open earlier. In spring, trails are often extremely wet and muddy. In autumn many days are sunny and warm, but the variability of the weather poses a new challenge, since snow may begin to accumulate over high passes.

### Town of Banff Hikes

★ **Cascade Amphitheater** You can't miss Cascade Mountain—the beautiful pyramid-shaped peak at the northeastern end of Banff Avenue. One of the most rewarding day hikes in the townsite area, this is a demanding outing that starts (and later finishes) at the Mount Norquay day lodge, and takes you into a high alpine cirque in a hanging valley with a lush carpet of subalpine wildflowers. The trail ends at a dramatic point on the south edge of the meadows, on a small knoll of rockslide debris. *7.7km (4.8 miles) each way. Strenuous. Elevation gain is 640m (2,100 ft.). 6 hrs round-trip. Trail head is Mount Norquay ski area. Map p 140.*

★ **C-Level Cirque** This trail has wonderful panoramic views and is a great afternoon getaway from busy Banff Avenue. After alighting on a stunning view of Lake Minnewanka, the trail heads back into the now-subalpine forest before ending in a small cirque (like a bowl with a circular ridge surrounding it) at the highest part of the valley. Look for calypso orchids, marmots, and pika as you climb to the treeless alpine zone. *3.9km (2.4 miles) each way. Moderate. Elevation gain 455m (1,493 ft.). 3 hrs round-trip. Trail head is Upper Bankhead picnic area parking lot, 3.5km (2¼ miles) on Minnewanka Rd. from the Minnewanka interchange on the Trans-Canada Hwy. Map p 140.*

**kids** **Sundance Canyon** A gentle hike that leaves from the Cave and Basin Historic Site is good in spring and fall. There are nice views of the Sawback Range and the pinnacle of Mount Edith. It goes up a paved trail, turning at Sundance Creek and continuing on to an extraordinary canyon with giant boulders. Head over the bridge and up the stairs for the best views. *4.3km (2.7 miles) each way. Easy. Elevation gain 143m (469 ft.). 3 hrs round-trip. Trail head at Cave and Basin Historic Site. Map p 140.*

### Bow Valley Parkway & Sunshine Meadows

**Castle Lookout** This hike gets you close to a former fire lookout on this scenic mountain. Short but steep, the trail offers an amazing panorama of the glacier-chiseled Bow Valley and Storm Mountain, which is often surrounded by its own gnarly weather system. This trail can be very warm on a sunny

*A hiker at Cory Pass.*

# Easy to Hard: Difficulty Ratings

Hiking times depend on a hiker's experience and fitness, as well as the weather conditions. Hikers of an average fitness level can usually hike 2.5 to 3.5km (1.6–2.2 miles) in an hour. Steeper trails will take longer, and you'll want to add in time for lunch, snack, and rest breaks.

**Easy** Hikes that are generally smooth and gentle, usually less than 6km (3.7 miles) long with an elevation gain of no more than 300m (984 ft.).

**Moderate** Hikes up to 13km (8 miles) long on well-established trails with some exposure. Elevation gain can be up to 600m (1,969 ft.).

**Difficult** Hikes longer than 13km (8 miles), with an elevation gain of more than 600m (1,969 ft.). Often on poorly defined trails, with obstacles and exposed terrain.

Lengths listed here are total distance from the start to the finish of the hikes. Elevation gain is the total ascent from the lowest point on the trail to the highest point.

day and is a great "shoulder season" choice. *3.7km (2.3 miles) each way. Strenuous. Elevation gain 520m (1,706 ft.). 3–4 hr. round-trip. Trail head is parking lot on the north side of the Bow Valley Pkwy. 1A, 5km (3 miles) west of Castle Junction. Map p 140.*

★ **Cory Pass** This is one of the most strenuous and challenging hikes in Banff, but it's also by far the most spectacular one near the Town of Banff. The highlight is the 2,300m (7,546-ft.) monolithic limestone cliffs of the Sawback Range. The trail starts in a high, subalpine valley bottom and ends in a high alpine zone well above the tree line—tremendous ecological diversity. Be sure to take a good map with you on this trail (see sidebar on p 145). *5.8km (3.6 miles) each way. Very strenuous. Elevation gain is 915m (3,002 ft.). 6–7 hr. round-trip. Trail head is Fireside Picnic Area at the eastern end of the Bow Valley Pkwy. 1A. Map p 140.*

**Ink Pots** Continue past the crowds at Johnston Canyon, passing the Upper Falls, twice the size of the lower ones. The trail opens into a lovely, wide valley and takes you to jade-colored natural springs. It's a magical place and very quiet after the rush of the canyon. *5.5km (3.4 miles) each way. Moderate. Elevation gain 243m (797 ft.). 4–5 hr. round-trip. Trail head is Johnston Canyon parking lot, 18km (11 miles) west of Banff on the Bow Valley Pkwy. 1A. Map p 140.*

★★ **kids Sunshine Meadows** Located high in an alpine bowl that is also the site of the Sunshine Village ski resort in winter, this alpine meadow is famous for its annual display of beautiful wildflowers, and is incredibly easy to get to—just take a shuttle to the Sunshine Village day lodge, where all trail heads are located. **White Mountain Adventures** (☎ 800/408-0005 or 403/762-7889; www.sunshinemeadowsbanff.com) runs a shuttle service to the area. *Map p 140.*

*A family hikes through autumn larches at Sunshine Meadows.*

The Rock Isle Lake trail leads you to the other side of the Continental Divide, into British Columbia's Mount Assiniboine Provincial Park. Rock Lake is particularly lovely in the calm early morning, when it mirrors the surrounding scenery, and the view stretches off into British Columbia's mountains. It's a favorite of artists and photographers. *2.5km (1.6 miles) each way. Easy. Elevation gain is 105m (344 ft.). 2 hr round-trip.*

The Simpson Pass/Healy Meadows trail is worth an afternoon outing for rewarding views of Wawa Ridge, Mount Assiniboine, and the Monarch, a massive pyramid-shaped

*The Lake Agnes Teahouse.*

peak. It's a wildflower-lover's dream, and a favorite of Banff's old outfitters and pioneers, including Jim Brewster and "Wild Bill" Peyto, two of Banff's original mountain guides. *7.6km (4.7 miles) each way. Moderate. Elevation gain is 160m (525 ft.). 5 hr. round-trip.*

### Lake Louise Hikes

★★ **Lake Agnes/Beehives** In a picturesque hanging valley above Lake Louise, Lake Agnes has been a favorite for more than a century. There are great views of the Bow Valley and wonderful history to be had at the Lake Agnes Teahouse on the shore of the lake, which serves

# Hiking To-Do List

1. **Select a trail.** Read through the hikes listed here, pick up a map and other hiking guides, and chat with the staff at the Banff Information Centre (224 Banff Ave.; ☎ 403/763-1550; www.pc.gc.ca/banff) or the Lake Louise Visitors Centre (Samson Mall, 101 Lake Louise Dr.; ☎ 403/522-3833) to get the right trail for you.

2. **Get a map.** The best are topographic maps, with a scale of 1:50,000. The Canadian government produces maps with lots of detail, but they are short on hiking trails. GemTrek Maps produces the best hiking maps in the Canadian Rockies. Pick one up in Banff or order at www.gemtrek.com. They're waterproof, tear-resistant, and have topographic contours, key for measuring elevation changes.

3. **Check the weather.** Get the up-to-date forecast by calling Banff National Park (☎ 403/762-1550) or Environment Canada in Banff at ☎ 403/762-2088.

4. **Check trail conditions.** Call the Park at ☎ 403/762-1550 for the latest trail reports, which are also posted around town and online at www.pc.gc.ca/banff.

5. **Bring plenty of water.** At least 1 liter (2 pints) of water per person, more if you're going on a strenuous full-day hike.

6. **Go in a group.** Some areas of Banff are under bear warnings and hikers must stay in groups of four or six at a time. It's safer, and often more fun!

7. **Tell someone about it.** Let someone know where you're going and when you'll be back.

freshly baked scones and tea throughout the summer. From the teahouse, take the trail to the north shore of the lake to connect with the Big Beehive. *5.1km (3.2 miles) each way. Moderate. Elevation gain is 400m (1,312 ft.). 4 hr. roundtrip. Trail head is Lake Louise shoreline trail, in front of the Fairmont Chateau Lake Louise. Map p 140.*

**kids** Lakeshore Trail This broad, flat trail may be the most well-trodden trail in Banff National Park. It leads you away from the crowds, around the north shore of the lake to the base of Mount Victoria and the shimmering Victoria Glacier.

There are many benches along the trail where you can sit and marvel at Lake Louise's color and beauty. Come early in the morning to beat the crowds. *1.9km (1.2 miles) each way. Easy. No elevation gain. 1 hr. round-trip. Trail head is in front of Fairmont Chateau Lake Louise. Map p 140.*

## Moraine Lakeshore Trail

Moraine Lake is a popular destination, but luckily this trail, along the western shore of the lake, is still a peaceful and pleasant way to enjoy the dramatic and imposing Valley of the Ten Peaks. The best views are at the start of the trail, but for a

*The rushing Paradise Creek in Paradise Valley.*

spectacular view of Moraine Lake at the end of the hike head 5 minutes up to the Moraine Lake Viewpoint, at the south end of the parking lot, following the sign to Consolation Lakes. *1.2km (.7 mile) each way. Easy. No elevation gain. 1hr round-trip. Trail head is Moraine Lake parking lot. Map p 140.*

### ★★★ Paradise Valley/Larch Valley

A rewarding and challenging full-day hike, you'll hike below mounts Temple and Lefroy, and past Lake Annette, Horseshoe Meadows, and the "Giant's Staircase" waterfall, then over Sentinel Pass and down through Larch Valley—all superb highlights. The trail ends at a different parking lot from where it begins, so you'll need to organize a shuttle. Parks Canada often requires hikers to stay in groups of six or more due to bear activity in the area. *17km (11 miles) each way. Strenuous. Elevation gain is 880m (2,887 ft.). 6–7 hr. Trail head is 2.5km (1½ miles) south on the Moraine Lake Rd. from Lake Louise Rd., in the Paradise Valley lot, on the right side of the road. Map p 140.*

### ★★ Plain of the Six Glaciers

If you have time for only one half-day hike in Lake Louise, take this route through postcard-worthy scenery as

it makes its way around Lake Louise and below mounts Victoria and Lefroy. It empties into a harsh glacier- and avalanche-scoured terrain before climbing into a lush meadow, where you can stop at the historic Plain of the Six Glaciers Teahouse. From the summit of a small moraine, you'll have the glaciers spread out before you. *5.3km (3.3 miles) each way. Moderate. Elevation gain 365m (1,198 ft.). 4–5 hr. round-trip. Trail head is Lake Louise*

*Hiking through the Plain of the Six Glaciers.*

*Shoreline trail in front of Fairmont Chateau Lake Louise hotel. Map p 140.*

**Saddleback Pass** The trail takes you to a stupendous view of the colossal Mount Temple from a pass between Saddle and Fairview mountains. Heading out along the lower slopes of Mount Fairview, the trail switchbacks up to a flower-filled meadow. It's steep, so bring poles to ease the trip down. Continue a bit farther to Fairview's summit for a mile-high view of Lake Louise. *3.7km (2.3 miles) one-way to pass. Moderate to strenuous. Elevation gain is 595m (1,952 ft.). 4 hr. round-trip. Trail head is on the south shore of Lake Louise to the right of the old guide's cabin. Map p 140.*

### Icefields Parkway Hikes

**kids Bow Glacier Falls** When the Bow Glacier retreated, it left behind a majestic 120m (394-ft.) waterfall that simply hints at the massive icefield above it. The trail is broad and scenic alongside the flats skirting Bow Lake, a Rocky Mountain gem. At the western shore of the lake there are views of the stunning Crowfoot and Bow glaciers. Only 100 years ago, the Bow Glacier extended to cover the entire Bow Valley. *4.7km (2.9 miles) each way. Easy. Elevation gain 95m (312 ft.). 3 hr. round-trip. Trail head is beside Num-Ti-Jah Lodge 36km (22 miles) north of the Lake Louise junction on Icefields Pkwy. 93. Map p 140.*

**★ Helen Lake** With tall peaks, alpine meadows, lakes, and wide views, this trail is diverse enough to draw you enthusiastically around every corner. This is a relatively quick and pain-free way to access the high alpine environment. The lakeside meadows draw friendly hoary marmots. Check out the view of the Crowfoot Glacier. *6km (3.7*

*A hiker crosses a creek at Helen Lake.*

*miles) each way. Moderate. Elevation gain 455m (1,493 ft.). 4 hr. round-trip. Trail head is across the highway from the Crowfoot Glacier Viewpoint, 33km (21 miles) north of the Lake Louise junction on Icefields Pkwy. 93. Map p 140.*

**★ Nigel Pass** On this rewarding hike that tops out on a rocky 2,195m (7,201-ft.) ridge marking the boundary between Banff and Jasper national parks, you'll have great views of the Columbia Icefield. East of the pass, you can scramble over rocks to catch sight of the Brazeau River and the waterfall along the rocky north wall of Nigel Pass. *7.2km (4.5 miles) each way. Moderate. Elevation gain 365m (1,198 ft.). 5 hr. round-trip. Trail head is 2.5km (1½ miles) north of the "Big Bend" switchback (114km/71 miles north of the Lake Louise junction) or 8.5km (5¼ miles) south of the Banff–Jasper boundary on the Icefields Pkwy. 93. Parking lot is on northeast side of the highway. Map p 140.*

**★★★ Parker Ridge** The best short day hike in the Icefields Parkway area, this high and open route takes you deep into the heart of the unforgiving alpine zone. In summer—which can last only a few weeks up here—the meadows turn

*A hiker crosses a creek at Helen Lake.*

a brilliant red with heather. Once you reach the summit, enjoy views of the Saskatchewan Glacier (the glacier that reaches the farthest out into a valley in the Columbia Icefield) below you. *2.7km (1.7 miles) each way. Moderate. Elevation gain 250m (820 ft.). 3 hr. round-trip. Trail head is in parking lot on the west side of the Icefields Pkwy. 93, 4km (2½ miles) south of the Banff–Jasper park boundary. Map p 140.*

**Peyto Lake/Bow Summit** This is the most popular short hike along the Icefields Parkway. Escape the

crowds by continuing on to the Bow Summit lookout; then hike down to the lake for an almost bird's-eye view of the Bow River's source. This trail takes you through what is known as the transition zone; what begins as a thick forest soon becomes a stunted one, getting sparser and sparser until you come to an area where there isn't a single tree growing. *3.1km (1.9 miles) each way. Easy. Elevation gain 230m (755 ft.). 2 hr. round-trip. Trail head is Bow Summit parking lot 41km (25 miles) north of the Lake Louise junction on Icefields Pkwy. 93. Map p 140.*

★★★ **Wilcox Pass** Starting just across the border in Jasper National Park, this trail gives you an almost bird's-eye view of the spectacular Columbia Icefields from the edge of a gorgeous alpine valley. It's an incredibly rewarding—albeit popular—trail since it's mostly above the treeline, offering nearly non-stop views and plenty of wildflowers in August. *12km (7.4 miles) return. Moderate. Elevation gain 335m (1,099 ft.). 5 hr. round-trip. Trail head is 2.5km (1.6 miles) south of the Icefields Centre on Icefields Pkwy. 93 at the Wilcox Pass campground. Map p 140.*

*A hiker pauses at Wilcox Pass, looking at the Columbia Icefields.*

# Backpacking: The Ultimate Rocky Mountain Experience

It's a challenging undertaking—most people just starting to backpack will find the routes in Banff National Park demanding because of the mountainous terrain. And you must be very well organized with what you bring on the trip. The peak hiking season is from early July to mid-September, and be sure to reserve your campsites ahead of time. There are dozens of possible trips, but the three listed here are my favorites!

## Backpacking Hikes

### ★★ Egypt Lake/Shadow Lake

This is the most popular backpacking area in Banff National Park, a multi-day exploration of Banff's highest-elevation hiking routes. With a series of passes along the Continental Divide, encompassing cliffs, meadows, and lake-dotted alpine cirques, this trail takes you through some quintessential Canadian Rockies landscape. *40km (25 miles) return. Moderate. Elevation gain 790m (2,592 ft.). 2–3 days. Trail head is Sunshine Village ski area. Map p 156.*

**kids Glacier Lake** This overnight trip isn't too strenuous and gets you into the Icefields Parkway backcountry. It's a nice outing for families, since the hike is quite flat and the elevation is relatively low. The beginning elevation is 1,450m (4,757 ft.) and you gain 210m (689 ft.) over the course of the trip. *8.9km (5.5 miles) each way. Easy. Elevation gain 210m (689 ft.). 2 days. Trail head is on west side of Icefields Pkwy. 93, 1.2km (¾ mile) north of the junction with Hwy. 11, near Saskatchewan Crossing. Map p 140.*

### ★★★ Sunshine Meadows/ Mount Assiniboine

Showcasing the spectacularly colorful Sunshine Meadows and Mount Assiniboine

*Hikers cross a bridge in Assiniboine Provincial Park.*

region, this route covers high alpine terrain, crosses dramatic passes, and runs alongside picturesque lakes. Head over Citadel Pass to admire Mount Assiniboine (the highest mountain in Banff National Park, also known as the "Matterhorn of the Rockies"). *62km (39 miles) return. Moderate to strenuous. Elevation gain 655m (2,149 ft.). 3–6 days. Trail head is Sunshine Village ski area. Map p 140.*

# Summer Sports

## Canoeing
**Moraine Lake 8**
**Lake Louise 5**
**Bow River at Banff 13**

## Biking
**Vermillion Lakes 11**
**Banff Springs Golf
   Course drive 18**
**Spray River Loop 21**
**Bow River Loop 4**

## Birdwatching
**Cave and Basin
   March 14**
**Fenland Trail 12**
**Bow River Bridge
   and Castle Junction 7**

## Climbing
**"Back of the Lake"
   at Lake Louise 3**
**Mount Athabasca 1**
**Mount Assiniboine 26**

## Fishing
**Vermillion Lakes 10**
**Upper Bow River 6**

## Golf
**Fairmont Banff
   Springs Golf course 19**

## Helicopter Tours
**Icefields Helicopter Tours 2**
**Alpine Helicopters 24**

## Horseback Riding
**Spray River 22**
**Martin Stables 15**

## Rafting
**Kicking Horse River 9**
**Kananaskis River 25**
**Bow River 17**

## Swimming
**Upper Hot Spring 20**
**Johnson Lake 23**
**Sally Borden Building 16**

There are many activities to choose from during summertime in Banff. This isn't a place for loungers. Besides hiking, give yourself a chance to sample a few of the adventures listed below. Get out and try something new!

## Biking

With more than 190km (118 miles) of mountain-bike trails and numerous options for road biking, Banff is a friendly place for two wheels. Bike season runs from May to October. Note that not all hiking trails are open to bikers.

You can rent both road and mountain bikes in Banff National Park at BacTrax Bike Rentals (225 Bear St.; ☎ 403/762-8177) and Adventures Unlimited (211 Bear St.; ☎ 403/762-4554), which also has kids' bikes, trailers, and strollers, too. In Lake Louise, rent bikes at Wilson Mountain Sports (see p 21).

Road Biking Good routes around the Banff Townsite area include the Banff Springs Golf Course drive and the Vermillion Lakes. When you head out from the townsite, take the Bow Valley Parkway (Hwy. 93A). There's much less traffic than on the Trans-Canada Highway (Hwy. 1). If you're up at Lake Louise, try the old Great Divide Road, which leads into Yoho National Park—a quiet ride through mountain scenery.

*Mountain bikers ride along the Benchland Trail in the late evening.*

## Mountain Biking

Mountain biking is permitted on only a select number of the trails in Banff National Park. You are subject to fines if you are caught biking on hiking-only trails. In the Banff Townsite area, the best ride for beginners and families is the 13km (7.8-mile) Spray River Loop. Near Lake Louise, families with kids will enjoy the

## Share the Trail

Bike trails in Banff National Park are also hiking and horseback-riding trails. Expect to encounter people using the trail in other ways. Ride in control and always be prepared to stop. Slow down when you come upon a hiker. A friendly greeting will make them aware of your presence. Bikes can spook horses. When passing a horse, let the rider know you are coming. If a horse approaches you, move to the side of the trail, stop your bike, and let the horse pass. If you have a chance to stop and chat a little, ask the rider about the trail conditions ahead.

*A woman climbs the "Back of the Lake" route at Lake Louise.*

to the Town of Banff include Cave and Basin March and Fenland Trail. Look for an osprey nest on the Bow River Bridge and Castle Junction.

### Canoeing

To canoe is to be Canadian, it is said. There are boathouses where you can rent canoes at both Moraine Lake and Lake Louise. The Moraine Lake Lodge's boathouse (14km/8¾ miles south of Lake Louise on Moraine Lake Rd.; ☎ 403/522-3733) rents canoes for $40 per hour. The Fairmont Chateau Lake Louise (111 Lake Louise Dr.; ☎ 403/522-3511) rents canoes for $55 per hour. In the Town of Banff, rent a canoe at the Bow River Canoe Rentals (end of Wolf St.; ☎ 403/762-3632) for $34 per hour, where you can paddle straight into the placid Vermillion Lakes.

Be prepared if you're planning on canoeing the Bow River; experience is recommended, particularly in the section between Castle Junction and Banff, where there's a Class III rapid. The paddle from Banff to Canmore is intermediate-level and requires route-finding skills.

relatively flat but very scenic 7.1km (4.4-mile) Bow River Loop, which leaves from the Lake Louise Campground. There are interpretive signs along the trail.

### Bird-Watching

Birding is a great activity for visitors of all ages. More than 260 species pass through the Canadian Rockies annually. Pick up a brochure from the Banff Information Centre in Banff Townsite (224 Banff Ave.; ☎ 403/762-1550). Great spots close

### Climbing & Mountaineering

Visitors to Banff who've taken the time and energy to learn the ropes

*Fly fishing on the Upper Bow River.*

*Banff Springs Hotel and the Banff Springs Golf Course.*

enjoy this highly technical sport. There are no specific regulations governing climbing or mountaineering in Banff National Park; however, Parks Canada does suggest you contact the Banff Warden's office (in Banff ☎ 403/762-1470; in Lake Louise ☎ 403/522-1220) for more information before you head out.

There are a number of excellent rock-climbing locations in Banff, including the "Back of the Lake," at Lake Louise. Classic mountain climbs include mounts Athabasca and Assiniboine—both are for experienced climbers only.

For advice on planning a climbing trip, contact the Alpine Club of Canada (☎ 403/678-3200; www.alpineclubofcanada.ca) or the Association of Canadian Mountain Guides (☎ 403/678-2885; www.acmg.ca). For private lessons and guiding, contact Canada's premier mountaineering school, Yamnuska Inc. (☎ 403/678-4164; www.yamnuska.com).

### Fishing

You need a permit to fish in Banff National Park. Pick one up at the Banff Information Centre in Banff Townsite (224 Banff Ave.; ☎ 403/762-1550). National Park fishing permits cost $10 daily. An annual permit costs $34. Vermillion Lakes is a very popular fishing spot, so not surprisingly there aren't too many fish left. Don't even bother trying to fish at Lake Louise—again, there are none left. The Bow River is one of the world's finest fly-fishing rivers and is the only area in Banff National Park open year-round.

Banff Fishing Unlimited (☎ 403/762-4936; www.banff-fishing.com) specializes in year-round fly-fishing, spin casting, and trophy lake-trout fishing. Their guides know all the secrets. Alpine Anglers (☎ 403/762-8223; www.alpineanglers.com) offers top-notch instruction in the mild sensibilities of fly-fishing on the pristine, turquoise waters of the Bow River.

### Golfing

The Fairmont Banff Springs Hotel's 27-hole Stanley Thompson Course is world famous (405 Spray Ave.; ☎ 403/762-6801). Recently upgraded, the course has three tee-offs and an amazingly scenic location along the Spray and Bow rivers, beneath Mount Rundle. It's expensive but legendary, and open to the public (you don't have to be a guest at the hotel to play a round). Course fees range from $149 in May and October and $219 from June through September, including cart. There's also a 9-hole course. Watch for geese and elk!

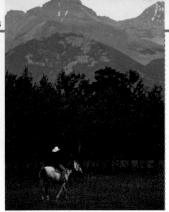

*Riding a horse near Banff.*

## Helicopter Tours

To get the ultimate bird's-eye view of the jaw-droppingly beautiful Rockies, you have to step just outside the boundary of Banff National Park. Near the Icefields Centre, Icefields Helitours (☎ 888/844-3514 or 403/721-2100; www.icefieldheli.com) takes those looking to splurge for a thrilling 55-minute chopper ride over the Columbia Icefield ($499). Alpine Helicopters (☎ 403/678-4802; www.alpinehelicopters.com) takes off just east of Banff in Canmore and flies to Mount Assiniboine and back in 30 unforgettable minutes ($249). They also have heli-hiking day tours starting at $389.

## Horseback Riding

Riding a horse in the Canadian Rockies is as logical as riding a camel in the Sahara Desert. Saddling up not only lets you explore the cowboy heritage of the Rockies, it also lets you wind your way into parts of the Banff backcountry you might not otherwise have seen. Having said this, only a select few trails in Banff National Park are able to accommodate horses, so I recommend taking a trip organized by a local outfitter. They'll show you a good ol' time, while keeping you on course.

Timberline Tours (☎ 403/522-3743; www.timberlinetours.ca) leads scenic trips at Lake Louise. A half-day outing is between $65 and $135, while an overnight trip is $390. Holiday on Horseback (132 Banff Ave., ☎ 800/661-8352 or 403/762-4551; www.horseback.com) has a corral at the Fairmont Banff Springs Hotel, where they run 1-hour tours along the Spray River ($40). They have another corral at Martin Stables (located on the banks of the Bow River across from Banff Townsite), where 5- to 7-hour trips head into the Sundance Range ($151–$188). They also organize wonderfully fun wilderness cook-outs, which include a Mountain Morning breakfast ride ($102) and an Evening Trailride, where they serve a large Western barbecue dinner ($102).

## Rafting

The gnarliest rapids in the Canadian Rockies are west of Banff on the Kicking Horse River (see p 150) and east of Banff on the Kananaskis River. From the Town of Banff, you can hop on a gentle float trip down

*Rafting down the Bow River.*

*Playing in the water at Johnson Lake.*

the Bow River. It's great for families. Rocky Mountain Raft Tours (☎ 403/762-3632; www.banffrafttours.com) departs from just below Bow Falls and drops you at Canmore for $84 for adults, $42 for youth 15 and under.

### Swimming

The spring-fed pools at the historic Banff Upper Hot Springs (see p 150) make for a memorable dip any time of year. On a hot summer day, join the locals for an afternoon swim at Johnson Lake on the Minnewanka Loop. Throughout the year, the nicest indoor pool in Banff is at the sunny Banff Centre's Sally Borden Centre (St. Julien Rd., ☎ 403/762-6450).

## Saddle Up & Head High

If you're not sure about long days of hiking and carrying your own packs but you still want to explore the backcountry of Banff, consider an overnight horseback trip. From early May to late October, trail rides range from 1 night to 1 week. Some outfitters combine guided trail rides with stays at rustic but comfortable backcountry lodges, while others include overnights in wilderness tents situated in truly spectacular settings. This is one of the best ways to see the back corners of Banff—with considerably less effort than backpacking. For trips from 2 to 4 days, ranging from $553 to $1,446, try **Holiday on Horseback** (132 Banff Ave.; ☎ 403/762-4551 or 800/661-8352; www.horseback.com). Starting at the Lake Louise Corral, **Timberline Tours** (☎ 403/522-3743; www.timberlinetours.ca) has overnight trips starting at $390 per person.

# Winter Sports

**Alpine Skiing**
**Lake Louise Resort 1**
**Mt. Norquay 13**
**Sunshine Village 14**

**Cross-Country Skiing**
**Golf Course Trail/**
**Spray River Loop 9**
**Moraine Lake Road 10**
**Pipestone 2**

**Dog Sledding**
**Spray Lakes 16**
**Divide Road 3**

**Ice Climbing**
**Yamnuska Inc. 15**
**Ice-Skating**
**Vermillion Lakes 7**
**Fairmont Banff**
**Springs Hotel 8**

**Lake Louise 4**

**Ice Walks**
**Johnston Canyon 12**

**Snowshoeing**
**Fenland Trail 6**
**Moose Meadows 11**
**Fairview Lookout 5**

**Winter is breathtaking in the Canadian Rockies**, in both beauty and temperature. Days can drop to −15 °C (5 °F) or lower, but you'll be too busy sampling the many adventures available—some you may have never experienced before—to care. Dress warmly, keep a pair of gloves nearby, and make the most of the sunny days and starry nights.

*A snowboarder at Mount Norquay.*

### Alpine Skiing

**Lake Louise Resort** The views here will have you picking your jaw up off the glistening powder snow. Easy to access and full of varied terrain, Louise keeps folks loyal. Beginners will find a friendly ski and snowboard school, as well as some lovely green runs to get started. Head straight to the top of the new Grizzly Express Gondola for more advanced blue runs. Larch is a great place for intermediates. Expert skiers should take to the Top of the World "Six-Pack" Chair then the Summit Platter and enjoy powder bowls like West Bowl and Boomerang. For snowboarders, there is a terrain park with jumps, obstacles, and railings. Cozy and rustic Temple Lodge, tucked in behind the resort below Whitehorn Mountain, is a good lunch restaurant. *Follow*

*Whitehorn Rd. off the Trans-Canada Hwy. 1 at the Lake Louise exit.* ☎ *800/258-7669 or 403/522-3555. www.skilouise.com.*

**Mount Norquay** At Banff's doorsteps, this small resort has produced many world-class ski racers. It's got plenty of steep runs, and it's intimate and convenient, particularly their economical ski-by-the-hour deals (starting with 2 hours), meaning you don't have to spend the entire day here to feel like you've gotten your money's worth. This is particularly appealing for beginners and families. On a powder day, head straight to the Memorial Bowl. It's open for night skiing on Fridays 5pm to 10pm. *At the end of Mount Norquay Dr.* ☎ *403/762-4421. www.banffnorquay.com.*

*A skier surveys Delirium Dive at Sunshine Village in Banff.*

**Sunshine Village** Tucked high in the alpine zone in a series of scenic bowls centered around a "village" with a hotel, day lodge, ski school, and gondola station, Sunshine gets fabulous snow and has an abundance of space. It stays open weeks later than the other resorts in Banff, usually until the third week of May. Strawberry and Standish chairs are great for beginners. The Continental Divide has amazing views for intermediate skiers. Goat's Eye Mountain is great for advanced skiers. And only experts need attempt the aptly named Delirium Dive. Advanced snowboarders will find a lot of flat terrain at Sunshine, but the terrain park has grown steadily over the years and is a fun spot for catching some air. *8km (5 miles) west of Banff Townsite at the end of Sunshine Rd.* ☎ *800/661-1676 or 403/762-6500.* *www.skibanff.com.*

**Cross-Country (Nordic) Skiing**
A wonderful way to explore the park in winter, cross-country skiing promises great exercise, views, and

## Ski Big Three

Ski packages that allow you to spend a day at each of Banff's three resorts are offered by the Ski Banff/Lake Louise partnership (P.O. Box 1085, Banff, AB T1L 1H9; ☎ 877/754-7080 or 403/762-4561; www.skibig3.com). Packages include hotel and lift tickets at each of the three resorts. The lift ticket prices for adults range from $240 for 3 out of 4 days to $480 for 6 out of 8 days. It's a great deal and an excellent way to sample Banff's outstanding skiing.

Rent downhill skis and equipment, as well as snowboarding equipment, in Banff at **The Ski Stop** (203A Bear St.; ☎ 403/762-1650) or at the Fairmont Banff Springs Hotel (405 Spray Ave.; ☎ 403/762-5333). In Lake Louise, rent skis, snowshoes, and snowboards at **Wilson Mountain Sports** (see p 21). For a ski or snowboard tune-up, try **Ultimate Ski and Ride** (206 Banff Ave.; ☎ 403/762-0547) or **Monod Sports** (see p 87).

solitude, if you're seeking it. There are more than 80km (50 miles) of managed trails in Banff National Park, many of them within a half-hour drive of Banff Townsite. The cross-country ski season runs from December to March.

Parks Canada regularly updates trail reports online at www.pc.gc.ca/banff and ☎ 403/762-1550 for Banff Townsite area or ☎ 403/522-3833 for Lake Louise.

Rent cross-country equipment at the Ski Stop (see p 150). In Lake Louise; rent skis and snowshoes at Wilson Mountain Sports (see p 21).

### Beginners

The Golf Course Trail has ungroomed trails that are wide open and easy for beginners. There are no defined trails and little elevation gain here, but it's a good place to get a feel for the sport. At Moraine Lake Road, there are 8km (5 miles) of double trackset trails, ideal for a good workout. Flat and wide, trails branch off to the west on the slopes of Mount Fairview.

### Intermediate

The Spray River Loop is a 12km (7.8 miles) trail leading behind the Fairmont Banff Springs Hotel with a 200m (656-ft.) elevation gain. Tracks are set for both skate-skiing and classic skiing. It's a good place if you want to go fast. The Pipestone Loops are a wide range of trails across the highway from the Lake Louise village, from 1.9 to 12km (1.2–7.8 miles). All are trackset. Check at the Lake Louise Visitors Centre for updates on trail conditions.

### Dog Sledding

Just over the border from Banff National Park, another classic winter tradition matches tourists up with friendly huskies for a mush across a frozen lake. It's exhilarating. Try Snowy Owl Sled Dog Tours (104-602 Bow Valley Trail, Canmore; ☎ 403/678-4369; www.snowyowltours.com). For mushing tours near Lake Louise, contact Kingmik Dog Sled Tours (☎ 403/763-8887; www.kingmikdogsledtours.com).

### Ice-Climbing

The frozen waterfalls of Banff National Park offer some of the finest ice climbing in the world. It's an extreme sport that requires proper preparation, but it's also an exhilarating experience—technical, exciting, and beautiful. Learn to climb with the guides at Yamnuska (☎ 403/678-4164; www.yamnuska.com).

*Cross-country skiing in front of the Chateau Lake Louise.*

# Steep & Deep Runs Near Banff

Within a few hours of the Town of Banff, there are two other amazing ski resorts worth a visit, both in the Columbia Valley in the Province of British Columbia next door. **Panorama Mountain Resort** (from Hwy. 95, turn west at Invermere and right onto Panorama Dr., 18km/11 miles to uphill; ☎ 800/663-2929 or 250/342-6941; www.panoramaresort.com) has a whopping 1,220 vertical meters (4,000 vertical ft.) and some deliciously long cruiser runs great for high-level intermediates. There's a cozy village of condos and hotels at the base. At **Kicking Horse Mountain Resort** (from Hwy. 95, turn west at blue sign in downtown Golden, 13km/8 miles uphill; ☎ 866/754-5425 or 250/439-5400; www.kickinghorseresort.com), the snow is famously so light it's called "Champagne powder." The resort will appeal mainly to advanced skiers who aren't intimidated by steep terrain and deep snow. The vibe is diehard and earthy.

### Ice-Skating

There are a number of places where you can skate outdoors under the winter sky. It's an exhilarating activity that's popular with families. Try the Vermillion Lakes, just outside the Town of Banff, in the early winter before the snow starts to pile up. There's also a public outdoor rink behind the Fairmont Banff Springs Hotel. At the Fairmont Chateau Lake Louise, there is an outdoor rink on the lake with a spectacular ice castle built right on top.

### Ice Walks

The frozen canyon walls at Johnston Canyon become a winter wonderland, thanks to ice cleats and the guides from Banff Adventures Unlimited (211 Bear St.; ☎ 403/762-4554; www.banffadventures.com), who take visitors out for a 4-hour discover of ice.

### Snowshoeing

Strapping a pair of snowshoes opens up miles and miles of possibilities in Banff, from short strolls near town to big backcountry bowls. Most snowshoe trails follow summer hiking trails—be sure to avoid cross-country trails (groomed or not groomed), as it interferes with the skiing. Near the townsite, try the flat Fenland Trail. You can snowshoe at Moose Meadows on the Bow Valley Parkway. More experienced snowshoers will work up a sweat at the Fairview Lookout above Lake Louise. ●

*An ice climber ascends Professor Falls in Banff.*

# The
# Savvy Traveler

# **Before** You Go

## Tourist Office

The Canadian Tourism Commission (☎ **604/638-8300**; www.canada. travel) and Travel Alberta, 999 8th St., Calgary (☎ 800/252-3782 or 780/427-4321; www.travelalberta. com) are useful sources of information. The Travel Alberta site is inspiring and helps you understand the breadth of attractions in this province. You can also check out the website for the Banff Lake Louise Tourism Bureau, Ste. 375, Cascade Plaza, Banff Ave. (☎ 403/762-8421; **www.banfflakelouise.com).**

## The Best Time to Go

Summer is the most enjoyable time of the year to be in the Canadian Rockies. However, it's also the most crowded and expensive time. Most hotels double their prices during the high season, which stretches from June through September. So consider the "shoulder seasons." In June, the days are luxuriously long and you can catch the early wildflowers in bloom and perhaps even some migrating caribou. In September, aspen and larch trees turn golden, but the midday temperature stays gloriously warm.

The Canadian Rockies are also a great destination in winter, by turns cozy, romantic, and peaceful, but also brimming with fun outdoor activities. Banff's star ski resorts—Sunshine Village, Mount Norquay, and Lake Louise—are among the best in North America. The main businesses in the Town of Banff stay open year-round, with many hotels dropping their prices substantially during the winter season, which runs from December to late March. There are often road closures throughout

*Previous Page: A welcome sign on the outskirts of Banff.*

the Canadian Rockies, especially in the high mountain passes.

## Festivals & Special Events

**JAN** Ice Magic Festival (☎ 403/762-8421; www.banfflakelouise.com) is a stellar ice-carving competition held on the frozen shores of Lake Louise.

**MARCH** Lake Louise Loppet (☎ 403/289-0386; www.calgaryskiclub.org) is a family-friendly annual cross-country ski race that also attracts Olympians and National Ski Team members.

**APRIL** Join the most radical freestyle skiers and snowboarders at Mount Norquay for the **Spring Fling Big Air Comp and Dummy Downhill** (☎ 403/762-7703; www.banff norquay.com).

**MAY** The Rocky Mountain Wine & Food Festival (☎ 866/228-3555; www.rockymountainwine.com) is held at the Fairmont Banff Springs Hotel. Sample from the best local bistros and a huge array of wine and spirits from around the world.

**MAY** Say farewell to winter with a splash at Sunshine Village's **Slush Cup Beach Party Weekend** (www. skibanff.com), the last weekend of the ski season. Outdoor concerts, a beer garden, and wild folks ski jumping across puddles are highlights.

**MAY–AUG** From drama and opera to jazz and classical music, the **Banff Summer Arts Festival** (☎ 403/762-6301; www.banffcentre.ca) showcases the best in a variety of artistic areas. If you are an arts lover, don't miss this.

**JUNE** Teams of 15 run the Icefields Parkway from Jasper to Banff as part of the annual **Banff to Jasper Relay** (www.bjr.ca).

**JUNE** A recent addition to the local events calendar, **the Banff National Park Bike Fest** (www.banfflakelouise.com) brings pedal power to the Rockies for a weekend of road races and fast-paced action.

**JULY** Held on July 1, **Canada Day** is the anniversary of the signing of the "North America Act" with Britain, which created the united country of Canada. Following a free pancake breakfast in Banff's Central Park, pick a good spot on Banff Avenue to take in the parade, with cowboys and marching bands. In the evening, there's live music in the park and fireworks light up the sky.

**AUG** Over the first weekend in August, the peaks form an amazing backdrop for 3 days of music at the annual **Canmore Folk Music Festival** (☎ 403/678-2524; www.canmore folkfestival.com), Alberta's longest-running folk music festival.

**AUG** Since 1926, Jasper has hosted the **Jasper Heritage Pro Rodeo** (☎ 780/852-4622; www.jasper heritagerodeo.com), featuring bareback, saddle bronc, steer wrestling, and barrel racing. There's a Western dance, barbecue, and kid's rodeo held in town.

**AUG** Banff's many heritage buildings welcome visitors during **Doors Open Banff** (☎ 403/762-8421; www.doorsopenalberta.ca) for self-guided heritage tours.

**SEPT** A Banff tradition that draws runners from across Western Canada, **Melissa's Road Race** (www.melissasroadrace.ca) has a 10K (6.2 mile) and 22K (13.7 mile) road route,

with proceeds going to the Banff community. It sells out months ahead of time, but spectators can catch the action at the finish line at the Banff Recreational Grounds.

**OCT–NOV** Each year, the Banff Centre hosts the **Banff Mountain Film and Book Festivals** (☎ 403/762-6301; www.banffcentre.ca) celebrating the spirit of those who live in the mountains. If you're a keen armchair adventurer, it's best to buy a weekend pass, which will get you into plenty of screenings as well as to hear guest speakers and attend the awards ceremony and closing party on Sunday evening.

**DEC** From a World Cup ski race to a Santa Claus Parade, winter gets a kick-start during the annual **Winter-Start Festival** (www.banfflake louise.com; ☎ 403/762-8421).

## The Weather

Despite the Canadian Rockies' northerly latitude, the climate actually resembles that of the Rocky Mountains south of the United States border because the altitude isn't as high as it is in the U.S. Rockies. Snow at lower elevations usually disappears by May, but sometimes hangs around the higher elevations well into the summer. Although it often rains for at least a week in June, and you can expect a cold rain or wet snowfall in July, the summer climate is generally very pleasant, with warm days and low humidity. Evenings almost always require a sweater. Rain clouds often gather along the Continental Divide, so don't be disappointed to come all the way here and not be able to see the high peaks right away. July temperatures typically hit 68° to 77°F (20°–25°C). Spring and fall days are

| AVERAGE MONTHLY TEMPERATURES & RAINFALL | | | | | | |
| --- | --- | --- | --- | --- | --- | --- |
| | JAN | FEB | MAR | APR | MAY | JUNE |
| High °F/°C | 23/–5 | 32/0 | 40/4 | 49/9 | 57/14 | 72/22 |
| Low °F/°C | 5/–15 | 13/–11 | 18/–8 | 27/–3 | 31/–1 | 41/5 |
| Days of precipitation | 12 | 10 | 11 | 11 | 13 | 14 |
| | JULY | AUG | SEPT | OCT | NOV | DEC |
| High °F/°C | 82/28 | 80/27 | 66/19 | 50/10 | 32/0 | 23/–5 |
| Low °F/°C | 45/7 | 44/7 | 38/3 | 31/–1 | 18/–8 | 7/–14 |
| Days of precipitation | 13 | 13 | 12 | 9 | 10 | 12 |

usually fine and bright, though evenings can be cool.

In January, though the lows can drop way down to –22°F (–30°C), the winter sunshine and blue skies are the stuff of legend.

## Useful Websites

In addition to the websites at the opening of this chapter, check out:

- **www.parkscanada.gc.ca**: Incredibly useful information on all of the area's national parks.

- **www.mountainnature.com**: Great information on the natural history of the area.

- **www.icefieldsparkway.ca**: A new, interactive website that offers a virtual tour of the of the world's most beautiful drives.

- **www.banff.com**: A site with events listings, virtual tours, weather updates, and listings for everything from restaurants to ski-rental shops.

- **www.banff.ca**: The site for the Town of Banff has useful information for visitors, including information on the public-transit system.

## Cellphones

The cellular phone coverage in the Canadian Rockies is spotty. In the Town of Banff, as in other towns like Canmore, Lake Louise, and Jasper, coverage is good. In between these spots, though, it is not reliable. For example, your coverage will likely cut out as you drive from Banff to Lake Louise. Phones using CDMA network technology—currently the most common type in use in both Canada and the U.S.—will work in Canada in places with reception. GSM/GPRS phones—the dominant standard pretty much everywhere else—also work here, thanks to roaming agreements. Before leaving home, be sure to update your phone's roaming software to assure good connectivity. And check with your provider to see what kind of international usage fees may apply. For information on land lines and international calls, see "Telephones", in the Fast Facts section below.

## Car Rentals

Most visitors to Banff and Jasper national parks will fly to either Calgary or Edmonton and rent a car to get to the parks. Though shuttle service is available from the Calgary International Airport to several locations around Banff (see the "By Plane," below), it's a good idea to rent a car to get around for the duration of your trip. For a list of agencies that operate in the area, see p 175.

# Getting **There**

## By Plane
Both the Calgary International Airport (☎ 877/254-7427 or 403/735-1200; www.calgaryairport.com) and the Edmonton International Airport (☎ 800/268-7134; www.edmonton airports.com) service the Canadian Rockies. If you are heading to Banff National Park, fly to Calgary and from there take either the Banff Airporter (☎ 888/449-2901 or 403/762-3330; www.banffairporter.com; $56 one-way or $106 round-trip), or Sundog Tours' (☎ 888/786-3641 or 403/762-2711; www.sundogtours.com; $55 to Banff, $72 to Lake Louise) airport shuttle, which is the only one that will take you to Lake Louise or Jasper from the Calgary Airport in both summer and winter.

Banff is 129km/80 miles west of Calgary. It's about 90 minutes by car from the airport.

If you want to visit Jasper National Park first, fly to Edmonton (363km/225 miles east of Jasper; a 4-hr. trip by car).

Many people visiting Jasper go first to Banff via Calgary and then drive north. Others do the trip in reverse.

## By Car
If you're driving into Banff National Park from the east, take the Trans-Canada Highway (Hwy. 1) west from Calgary. The Park's eastern gate is 129km (80 miles) west of the Calgary International Airport, just west of the town of Canmore. If you are coming to Banff from the west, you have two options. From central British Columbia, you can take the Trans-Canada Highway east via the town of Golden, BC, and Yoho National Park, and enter Banff just west of the village of Lake Louise.

The other option, from southeastern British Columbia, is to take Hwy. 93 north into Banff via the town of Radium Hot Springs, BC, and Kootenay National Park. See chapter 5 for more information on planning a side trip to Golden, BC, or Radium Hot Springs, BC.

If you're approaching the parks from the city of Edmonton, which is to the north, you'll get to Jasper National Park first. Take Hwy. 16 (the Yellowhead Hwy.) west to Jasper National Park's eastern gate (363km/225 miles west of Edmonton International Airport). From north-central British Columbia, you can take Hwy. 16 east to Jasper National Park via Prince George, BC, and Mount Robson Provincial Park.

Vancouver is 858km (532 miles) west of Banff and 863km (535 miles) west of Jasper.

## By Train
VIA Rail Canada (☎ 888/842-7245; www.viarail.ca) services Jasper National Park on its Edmonton–Vancouver run, which takes about 16 hours direct. Most trains from major Canadian and U.S. centers connect to this route. Check with VIA Rail Canada or with Amtrak (☎ 800/872-7245; www.amtrak.com).

There is no VIA Rail Canada service to Banff or Calgary; however, Rocky Mountaineer Railtours (☎ 877/460-3200; www.rocky mountaineer.com) has a stunning overnight trip that departs from Vancouver and stops in either Banff or Jasper (you select your destination at the changeover in Kamloops, BC). Royal Canadian Pacific Luxury Rail Tours (☎ 877/665-3044; www.royalcanadianpacific.com) has a 6-day tour on a luxury heritage rail car that leaves Calgary, passes through the Canadian Rockies south of Banff, and loops back through Golden and Banff to Calgary.

### By Bus

Greyhound Bus Lines (☎ 800/661-8747; www.greyhound.ca) and Brewster (☎ 877/791-5500; www.brewster.ca) have daily trips from Vancouver to Edmonton and Jasper, including a 2-day drive that includes an overnight stop mid-way. Their routes from Vancouver to Calgary stop in Canmore, Banff, Field, and Golden.

# Getting **Around**

### By Shuttle

There are a number of shuttle services to help ease your travel between Banff and Jasper national parks. Sundog Tours (☎ 888/786-3641 or 780/852-4056; www.sundogtours.com) runs between Banff, Lake Louise, and Jasper daily (except on poor winter-driving days and from Nov through late Dec). Some daily departures hit all the major attractions along the way; others go directly from Jasper to Lake Louise or Banff. The Jasper–Banff trip costs $59 per adult and $35 per child 12 and under; the Jasper–Lake Louise trip costs $53 per adult and $29 per child. Brewster (☎ 877/791-5500 or 403/762-6700; www.brewster.ca), the original tour company in Banff and Jasper, has a slew of shuttle services and day tours between Banff, Jasper, Calgary, and Edmonton, including a 9[bf]1/2-hour day trip that starts in Banff and ends in the Town of Jasper. It costs $134 for adults and $67 for children ages 5 to 15. Children under age 5 ride free.

### By Car

If you are staying in the Town of Banff and not really planning on trips outside of it, you can take a shuttle from the Calgary airport and then walk, take the local ROAM public bus system, or a short cab ride to most attractions in town. However, if you plan on seeing any of the rest of the park, including Lake Louise, as well as making a trip to Jasper, then having your own vehicle is a major advantage.

There is little to no public transport between main destinations in the Canadian Rockies, and shuttles and taxi services are very expensive—not to mention restricting, since your movements are governed by their schedule. The roads are in good condition most of the year (you don't really need to rent an expensive four-wheel-drive sport-utility vehicle except during major snowstorms), and driving here is a relaxing way to soak up the gorgeous scenery.

The one down side of renting a car is that parking can be a problem in the Town of Banff and at Lake Louise. Stick to the big parking lots (in Banff there is a covered multi-story parkade on Bear St. btw. Caribou and Buffalo sts., in Lake Louise at the Samson Mall, and in Jasper beside the Heritage Railway Station). For more information, see chapter 4.

### By RV

They're not for everyone, but most people who try it discover what a joy it is to travel by recreational vehicle. It affords a level of independence and comfort that car travel can't. And finding a quiet campground by a river is as close to the camping experience as you can get without giving up your pillow and mattress.

More than half of the campgrounds in Banff and Jasper national parks accommodate RVs, trailers, and camper vans, and you must stay in these designated areas. In addition to navigating around campgrounds, RVs (and their drivers) need to know how to get around town, too. In the town of Banff, there is a trailer drop-off site in the industrial area at the northeast end of Banff Avenue. You can leave your trailer here and take the car or RV itself through the streets of town. There are also a number of larger parking lots that accommodate RVs, including one near the Mineral Springs Hospital on Gopher Street and another one across from the post office on Buffalo Street, along the Bow River.

Many people come to the Rockies in an RV they've rented at the airport in Edmonton or Calgary.

Contact CanaDream (2510 27th St. NE, Calgary, AB T1Y 7G1; ☎ 800/461-7368 or 403/291-1000; www.canadream.com).

# Fast **Facts**

**ATMS**   Banff does have its share of Automated Teller Machines, which operate on the worldwide **Cirrus** (☎ 800/424-7787; www. mastercard.com), **PLUS** (☎ 800/843-7587; www.visa.com), and **Interac** (☎ 416/362-8550; www.interac.ca) networks. Be sure you know your personal identification number (PIN) before you leave home, and be sure your daily withdrawal limit will cover the amount of cash you'll need. Note that ATM fees can be higher for international transactions than for domestic. **Alberta Treasury's** branch is at 317 Banff Ave. (☎ 403/762-8505). In Lake Louise there is an ATM in Samson Mall (☎ 403/522-3678). The **Bank of Montreal** is at 107 Banff Ave. (☎ 403/762-2275), and the **Canadian Imperial Bank of Canada** (CIBC) is at 98 Banff Ave. (☎ 403/762-3317).

**BANKING HOURS**   Banks are generally open Mon–Fri 9:30am–4:30pm, though some branches have hours on weekends as well.

**BIKE RENTALS**   Bike shops will likely try to rent you their most expensive bikes. If you're a beginner mountain biker, however, and will only be heading out on a few trails around town, you do not need a full-suspension bike. If you want to just cruise the main, paved, trails of the townsite, go for an inexpensive bike.

You can rent both road and mountain bikes in Banff National Park at BacTrax Bike Rentals (225 Bear St.; ☎ 403/762-8177). Guided tours of the Vermillion Lakes and Sundance Canyon leave daily. In addition to renting regular-size bikes for adult riders, Adventures Unlimited (211 Bear St.; ☎ 403/762-4554) rents kids' bikes, trailers, and strollers, too. In Lake Louise, rent bikes at Wilson Mountain Sports (Samson Mall; ☎ 403/522-3636). In Jasper, the folks at Freewheel Cycle (681 Patricia St.; ☎ 780/852-3898; www. freewheeljasper.com) are the local experts on two-wheeling. They rent front-suspension mountain bikes that can also be used on roads. You can rent both road and mountain bikes from Jasper Source for Sports (406 Patricia St.; ☎ 780/852-3654).

**BUSINESS HOURS**   Hours vary by shop, but as a general rule most open daily around 10am and stay open until at least 6pm. Shops in the Town of Banff usually stay open later. Most are open daily, though some close on Sunday.

**CONSULATES & EMBASSIES** The **U.S. Consulate** is at Ste. 1000, 615 Macleod Trail SW, Calgary (☎ 403/266-8962). The **British Consulate** is at Ste. 700, 205 5th Ave SW, Calgary (☎ 403/705-1755). The **Irish Consulate** is at 3803 8th A St. SW., Calgary (☎ 403/243-2970). The **Australian Consulate** is at 2050 1075 W. Georgia St., Vancouver (☎ 604/684-1177). The consulate of **New Zealand** is at 888 Dunsmuir St., Ste. 1200 (☎ 604/684-7388).

**CURRENCY EXHANGE** Currency exchange counters can be found at the airport, but you'll get a better rate just using ATMs (see p 167) or at the **Custom House Global Foreign Exchange,** at 211 Banff Ave. (☎ 403/760-6630).

In Jasper, there is a currency exchange house in **Whistlers Inn** (105 Miette Ave.; ☎ 780/852-3361). Be sure to check current exchange rates before your trip via www.xe.com or any of the other major currency trackers.

**CUSTOMS** Non-Canadian residents will pass through **Canada Border Services** (☎ 800/461-9999 or 204/983-3500; www.cbsa-asfc.gc.ca) upon arrival. If you're concerned about items you intend to bring into the country, check the website's "Information for Visitors" section. U.S. citizens will pass through **U.S. Customs** (☎ 877/CBP-5511 [227-5511]; www.cbp.gov) on departure from Canada. The standard personal duty-free allowance for U.S. citizens returning from Canada is US$800. There are also limits on the amount of alcoholic beverages (usually 1L), cigarettes (1 carton), cigars (100 total, and no Cubans), and other tobacco

products you may include in your personal duty-free exemption. **Joint Customs declarations** are possible for family members traveling together. For instance, for a husband and wife with two children, the total duty-free exemption would be US$3,200. Note that most meat or meat products, fruits, plants, vegetables, or plant-derived products will be seized by U.S. Customs agents unless they're accompanied by an import license from a U.S. government agency.

For more specifics, visit the **U.S. Customs Service** website (www.customs.gov). U.K. citizens should visit the **U.K. Customs and Excise** site (www.hmce.gov.uk), Australians should go to the **Australia Customs Service** (www.customs.gov.au), Kiwis should check the **New Zealand Customs Service** (www.customs.govt.nz), and citizens of Ireland should check the **Irish Revenue** site (www.revenue.ie).

**DENTISTS** Most major hotels have a dentist on call. **Banff Dental Care** is at 210 Bear St. (☎ 403/762-3979). Call first for an appointment. The clinic is open Monday, Wednesday, Thursday, and Friday 8am to 5pm and Tuesday 9am to 6pm.

**DINING** Eating out will be one of your highlights in Banff. For the most popular spots, reservations are recommended, and are essential on Saturday evenings or long weekends.

**DOCTORS** Hotels usually have a doctor on call. **Alpine Medical Clinic,** 201A-211 Bear St. (☎ 403/762-3155), is a drop-in clinic open Monday through Thursday 8:30am to 7pm, Friday 8:30am to 5pm, and weekends 9am to 5pm.

**ELECTRICITY** Outlets and voltage (110 volts AC) are the same in Canada as in the United States, so laptops, chargers, hair dryers, and other small appliances from the U.S. will work just fine. Appliances from other countries will require an adapter and/or converter.

**EMBASSIES**  See "Consulates & Embassies" above.

**EMERGENCIES**  For emergencies in the Canadian Rockies, dial ☎ **911.**

**EVENT LISTINGS**  Event listings are posted online by the **Banff–Lake Louise Tourism Bureau** at www. banfflakelouise.com. The free local weekly newspaper **Rocky Mountain Outlook** (www.rmoutlook.ca) also is a great source for updated arts, sports, and community events. It's published on Thursdays and available throughout Banff.

**FAMILY TRAVEL**  Banff and the Canadian Rockies are fantastically kid-friendly. Family travel websites include **Family Travel Forum** (www.familytravelforum.com), a comprehensive site that offers customized trip planning; **Family Travel Network** (www.familytravel network.com), an online magazine providing travel tips; and **Travel-withyourkids.com** (www.travel withyourkids.com), a comprehensive site written by parents for parents offering sound advice for long-distance and international travel with children.

**GAY & LESBIAN TRAVELERS**  **Mountain Pride** (☎ 800/958-9621; www. gaybanff.com) is a social networking group for Banff residents and visitors. **Banff Gay Weddings** (☎ 403/609-3896; www.banffgay weddings.com) organizes same-sex ceremonies and events. While Alberta is perhaps the most conservative province in Canada, Banff and its neighboring towns are gay-friendly.

**HOLIDAYS**  Alberta has 12 public holidays throughout the year, when banks, government offices, schools, and some shops are closed: New Year's Day (Jan 1), Family Day (third Mon in Feb), Good Friday (the Fri before Easter), Easter Monday (the day after), Victoria Day (the Mon before May 25), Canada Day (July 1), Heritage Day (first Mon in Aug), Labor Day (first Mon in Sept), Thanksgiving (second Mon in Oct), Remembrance Day (Nov 11), Christmas (Dec 25), and Boxing Day (Dec 26).

**INSURANCE**  The cost of travel insurance varies widely, depending on the destination, the cost and length of your trip, your age and health, and the type of trip you're taking. You can get estimates from various providers through **InsureMyTrip. com.** Enter your trip cost and dates, your age, and other information, for prices from more than a dozen companies.

**Medical Insurance:** Most U.S. health plans do not provide coverage outside of the U.S., and the ones that do often require you to pay for services upfront and reimburse you only after you return home. As a safety net, you may want to buy travel medical insurance from providers like **MEDEX Assistance** (☎ 410/453-6300; www.medexassist.com) or **Travel Assistance International** (☎ 800/821-2828; www.travel assistance.com).

**Trip-Cancellation Insurance:** Trip-cancellation insurance typically covers you if you have to back out of a trip (due to illness, etc.), if your travel supplier goes bankrupt, if there's a natural disaster, or if your government advises against travel to your destination. Some plans cover cancellations for any reason. **TravelSafe** (☎ 888/885-7233;

www.travelsafe.com) offers both types of coverage. **Expedia** (www.expedia.com) also offers any-reason cancellation coverage for its air-hotel packages. Other recommended insurers include: **Access America** (☎ 866/807-3982; www.accessamerica.com); **Travel Guard International** (☎ 800/826-4919; www.travelguard.com); **Travel Insured International** (☎ 800/243-3174; www.travelinsured.com); and **Travelex Insurance Services** (☎ 888/457-4602; www.travelex-insurance.com).

**Lost-Luggage Insurance:** If your luggage is lost, immediately file a lost-luggage claim at the airport, detailing the luggage contents. Most airlines require that you report delayed, damaged, or lost baggage within 4 hours of arrival. On international flights, baggage coverage is limited to approximately US$9.07 per pound, up to approximately US$635 per checked bag. If you plan to check items more valuable than what's covered by the standard liability, see if your homeowner's policy covers your valuables, or get baggage insurance as part of your comprehensive travel-insurance package.

**INTERNET ACCESS**   Almost all hotels in the Canadian Rockies now provide some kind of Internet access, either wireless, wired, or via a business center. There are also free Wi-Fi hot spots in many locations around town, often in coffee shops.

**LIQUOR LAWS**   The legal drinking age in Alberta is 18. In British Columbia it is 19. Bars, lounges, and restaurants that serve alcohol all close between midnight and 2am, depending on when they got their liquor license. Government-operated liquor stores have a near monopoly on the sale of hard liquor, and also stock beer and wine.

Privately owned specialty wine stores (see p 86 for some of the best) mostly stick to the grape, but usually also carry a small selection of beer and spirits.

**LOST PROPERTY**   Lost items are often turned in to the **Town of Banff,** where they are kept for 30 days. Contact ☎ 403/762-1218 daily between 8am and 6pm for inquiries. There is also an online Lost Property Report available at the Town's website, www.banff.ca. Outside the Town of Banff, try **Parks Canada** at ☎ 403/762-1550.

If you lose your passport, contact your country's embassy or consulate immediately (see "Consulates & Embassies," above).

**MAIL & POSTAGE**   Mailing a letter within Canada costs 54¢. To the U.S., it's 98¢. To all other international destinations, it's $1.65. The main **post office** in Banff is at 204 Buffalo St. (☎ 403/762-2586; www.canadapost.ca), across from Central Park. You can also buy stamps at many drugstores and convenience stores.

**MONEY**   Canada's money is denominated the same as U.S. dollars, except its C$1 and C$2 denominations are coins rather than bills. The C$1 coin is known as a "loonie" as it has the image of a common loon on one side. The C$2 coin is known as a "toonie," for obvious comedic reasons. For exchange rates, see "Currency Exchange," p 168.

**NEWSPAPERS & MAGAZINES**   The major newspapers in Alberta are the *Calgary Herald* (www.calgaryherald.com), which publishes Mon–Sun, and the *Edmonton Journal* (www.theprovince.com), which publishes 7 days a week.

The local weekly newspapers in Banff are **The Rocky Mountain Outlook** (www.rmoutlook.ca), which publishes every Thursday, and **the Banff Crag and Canyon** (www.banffcragandcanyon.com), which hits stands on Tuesdays.

**PARKING** See "Getting Around: By Car," p 166

**PASSPORTS** U.S. citizens traveling to Canada by any means—air, sea, car, bus, train, or on foot—will need a passport but no visa. The same applies for citizens of Great Britain, Australia, Ireland, and New Zealand. If you're a citizen of another country, check the **Canada Border Services Agency** website, www.cbsa-asfc.gc.ca/travel-voyage, for specific requirements.

For safety, make two photocopies of your passport before leaving home. Take one set with you as a backup (keeping it separate from the original) and leave one at home.

**PERMITS** Every visitor to a national park is required to have a permit (also known as a pass). You can pick one up at a park gate or information center inside the parks. Permits are valid in all Canadian Rocky Mountain national parks (Banff, Jasper, Yoho, Kootenay, Waterton Lakes, and Glacier national parks). A day pass costs $9.80 for adults, $8.30 for seniors, and $4.90 for children. More economical is the Annual Pass, which is a good idea if you're planning to stay for a few days and visit more than one park. It's valid for 1 year from the purchase date for unlimited entries to every one of Canada's national parks, coast to coast. Individual rates are $68 for adults, $58 for seniors, and $33 for children ages 6 to 12. The pass is free for children under age 6. For groups of 2 to 7, this pass costs $136, making it the best deal for most visitors.

Permits are also required for backcountry camping and fishing inside the National Parks. For more information visit www.pc.gc.ca

**PET-FRIENDLY TRAVEL** While there are a few hotels in Banff that welcome pets, in general the Canadian Rockies aren't particularly pet-friendly. This is mainly due to the importance placed on the health of the local wildlife populations. Keep your dog on a leash at all times, especially in campgrounds and on hiking trails. To wildlife like elk, wolves, bears, and cougars, your dog may look an awful lot like dinner. Avoid any areas in the parks where the potential for wildlife encounters is high (ask at an information center), and take your dog for a walk only during daylight hours. Do not leave your dog unattended outside. Unrestrained pets have been known to harass wildlife, provoke attacks, and endanger people. And please pick up after your pooch—the "leave no trace" principle applies to pets, too.

**PHARMACIES** The biggest pharmacy in the Town of Banff is **Rexall Drug Store,** lower level of Cascade Plaza, 317 Banff Ave., ☎ **403/762-2245.**

**POLICE** Call ☎ **911** for emergencies.

**SAFETY** Don't drink the water from any streams, rivers, or lakes in Banff or Jasper national parks. A waterborne parasite called *Giardia lamblia* can cause an illness known in Canada as "beaver fever." It is transmitted via infected animal feces and can cause serious and prolonged gastrointestinal problems.

Also be on the lookout for wood ticks—small, flat-bodied, spider-like insects that bite humans and can carry Rocky Mountain spotted fever and Lyme disease (although the latter is rare in the northern Rockies). They usually abound in dry, grassy slopes in the spring. If you're hiking through such an area, give yourself a good once-over at the end of the day. If in doubt, drop by the Mineral

Springs Hospital in Banff to see a doctor (301 Lynx St.; ☎ 403/762-2222). In Jasper, go to Seton General Hospital (518 Robson St.; ☎ 780/852-3344). There has been no evidence of West Nile virus in the Canadian Rockies.

Hiking in the mountains is so beautiful that it may make you feel lightheaded. But lightheadedness may also be a sign of altitude sickness. Although elevations in the Canadian Rockies aren't as high as in the Colorado and Montana Rockies, you can still feel the altitude. People with severe heart or lung conditions should take note. Others should bring along some headache medicine and drink plenty of water.

You'll also be closer to the sun in the mountains, so wear a sun hat and sunscreen. Beyond the sun, cold and rain are the other weather factors that could hamper your holiday. Check the latest weather forecast before heading out. Always pack a rain jacket and warm clothing in your daypack. And always carry a first-aid kit, both in your car and in your pack. At the very least, it should include latex gloves (to prevent spreading infections), butterfly bandages, sterile gauze pads, adhesive tape, antibiotic ointment, pain relievers (for kids and adults), alcohol pads, knife, scissors, and tweezers.

In terms of personal safety in the mountains, be aware that almost any slope is a potential avalanche chute—and even small avalanches can be deadly. Drivers should avoid stopping in places where there are signs that read NO STOPPING, AVALANCHE AREA, and anyone venturing into the backcountry—especially in winter—should know how to recognize and travel in avalanche terrain. Call ☎ 403/762-1460 in Banff or ☎ 780/852-6176 in Jasper for the latest avalanche hazard reports from Parks Canada.

There is also a risk of getting hit by falling rock and ice or slipping into a glacier crevasse, particularly in Jasper National Park. Do not ignore the signs telling you to stay back from the Angel Glacier at Mount Edith Cavell or the Athabasca Glacier, both in Jasper. These can be—and have been—deadly.

Don't leave valuables in your car or unattended in public places. This also applies to hiking trail heads. The Canadian Government website (**www.safecanada.ca**) has a list of safety tips in case you need something to worry about.

**SENIOR TRAVELERS** Shops, hotels, attractions, and services throughout Western Canada often offer discounts for people over 65.

**SMOKING** Smoking is prohibited in all public places in Alberta and British Columbia, including bars, clubs, and restaurants.

**TAXES** All hotels, restaurants, gift shops, and services charge the 5% goods and services tax (GST) on all purchases. (*Note*: A program that allowed foreigners to receive a rebate for the GST spent during their time in Canada was cancelled in 2007.) There is no provincial sales tax in Alberta. In British Columbia, a provincial sales tax of 7% is charged on purchased goods.

**TELEPHONES** **Dialing within Alberta** requires you to use full 10-digit phone numbers, including the area code, of which there are two in Alberta: 403 and 780. To reach the British Columbia side of the Canadian Rockies, first dial 250. **Phoning between the U.S. and Canada** requires no special trick: Just dial 1 plus the area code and local number, as you would between states in the U.S. **To dial other countries** direct from Banff, dial the international access code

(011), followed by the relevant country code (61 for Australia, 353 for Ireland, 64 for New Zealand, and 44 for the U.K.) and the local number with area code, if applicable. **To call Banff from outside North America,** dial the international access code (00 from the U.K., Ireland, or New Zealand, or 0011 from Australia), the country code (1), and then the local number with area code. For information on cellphone service, see "Cellphones," p 164.

**TIME ZONE** Alberta and the B.C. Rockies are located in the Mountain time zone, 7 hours behind Greenwich Mean Time (changing to the Pacific time zone between Golden and Revelstoke). The area observes daylight saving time from the second Sunday in March to the first Sunday in November.

**TIPPING** Customary tipping amounts are the same in Banff and the rest of Canada as in major U.S. cities, with a target of 15% for restaurants and taxis. (Though many people round that up to 20%.) If porters help with you bags at hotels or airports, the usual tip is $1 per bag (or $2 if it's heavy).

**TOILETS** Public toilets are increasingly easy to find in Banff. In fact, there are now nine facilities dotted around the main area of town, including the Whyte Museum, the Public Library, and Cascade Plaza. You can also find facilities at the corner of Wolf Street and Banff Avenue, and in the Parks Canada Administration Building, just across the Bow River Bridge. In Lake Louise, there are facilities in the Visitor Centre, in the main parking lot at the lakeshore, and in the Fairmont Chateau Lake Louise.

**TOURIST OFFICES** The following on-the-ground tourist centers can help with information, maps, suggestions, and booking accommodations: **Banff Information Centre** is at 224 Banff Ave. (☎ 403/762-1550), and there is a similar location at the **Lake Louise Visitor Centre,** in Samson Mall, 101 Lake Louise Dr. (☎ 403/522-3833). **Jasper National Park's Information Centre** is at 500 Connaught Dr. (☎ 780/852-6716). Just before you enter Banff National Park, you can visit the **Travel Alberta Visitor Information Centre** in Canmore at 2801 Bow Valley Trail (☎ 800/252-3782 or 403/678-5277), which is right off the Trans-Canada Highway 1.

**TOURS** Brewster (P.O. Box 1140, Banff, AB T1L 1J3; ☎ 877/791-5500 or 403/762-6700; www.brewster.ca) knows Banff better than any other tour operator and has a long history of guiding here to prove it. It offers many sightseeing tours in both Banff and Jasper. Taking even the 3-hour **Discover Banff with Banff Gondola tour** will teach you more than you'll ever learn on your own. If you're going to British Columbia, sign up for Brewster's **Rockies Discovery** 3-day, 2-night tour that stops in Calgary, Banff, Lake Louise, Roger's Pass, and Kamloops.

Discover Banff Tours (215 Banff Ave., P.O. Box 1566, Banff, AB T1L 1B5; ☎ 877/565-9372 or 403/760-5007; www.banfftours.com) leads small groups on interpretive tours of all the highlights in Banff National Park, including the Town of Banff, Lake Louise, and Moraine Lake, as well as the Icefields Parkway. Morning and evening wildlife-viewing tours are really nice.

**TRAVELERS WITH DISABILITIES** The museums and visitor centers in Banff are all wheelchair-accessible. Most hotels now have at least one wheelchair-accessible room. The Upper Hot Springs in Banff National Park and the Radium Hot Springs in Kootenay National Park are friendly to those with mobility restraints.

If you are planning on car camping, head for Tunnel Mountain, Johnston Canyon, Lake Louise, or Waterfowl Lakes campgrounds. In Jasper National Park, try Whistlers, Wapiti, or Wabasso.

Signs clearly mark which trails in the parks are paved. In Banff, try the asphalt-covered Sundance Trail. There is an adjustable-height viewing scope at Bow Summit. The Lakeside Trail at Lake Louise is another wheelchair-accessible trail. Wheelchair-friendly trails in Jasper include the Clifford E. Lee Trail at Lake Edith/Annette and the Maligne Lake Trail, as well as points along Maligne Canyon, at Pyramid Island, and the interpretive loop at the Pocahontas Coal Mine Trail.

**WEIGHTS & MEASURES** Canada uses the metric system. Remember: 1km=0.62 miles, 1 liter=0.26 gallons, 1 kilogram=2.2 pounds, and Celsius temperatures are based on 0 being the freezing point (in Fahrenheit measurement it's 32).

# A Brief **History**

**175 MILLION YEARS AGO** The Rocky Mountains are formed as the Pacific tectonic plate moves under the North American plate.

**11,000 B.C.** Early archeological records date the presence of peoples like the Crees, Kootenays, and Plains Blackfoot to have lived, fished, and hunted in the vast Rocky Mountains.

**1754** The first recorded visit of a European to the Rockies is made by Anthony Hendy.

**1800** Legendary explorer and mapmaker David Thompson explores the Bow Valley.

**1841** George Simpson, the Governor of the Hudson's Bay Company, is the first known European to visit the Town of Banff area.

**1871** As part of a deal to unite British Columbia with the rest of Canada, the Canadian government forms the Canadian Pacific Railway (CPR) to construct a railway across the new nation.

**1882** Tom Wilson, a CPR guide, becomes the first non-Native man to see Lake Louise, with the help of his Stoney partner.

**1883** Three railway workers stumble upon a series of hot springs on the lower slopes of Sulphur Mountain.

**1885** Canada's first national park is formed in Banff, preserving 26 sq. km (10 sq. miles) surrounding the hot springs. The reserve is increased to 670 sq. km (259 sq. miles) in 1887 and 7,125 sq. km (2,751 sq. miles) in 1917.

**1886** Construction of the Canadian Pacific Railway is completed. Banff is named after the Scottish district "Banffshire," birthplace of two of the CPR's directors, Lord Strathcona and George Stephen.

**1888** The CPR opens the elegant log-framed 250-room Banff Springs Hotel, the most expensive hotel in the world at the time.

**1890** A log cabin is built on the shores of Lake Louise, soon to be replaced by a larger "chateau."

**1917** The Federal Government passes the first National Parks Act in the world.

**1921** A road is completed linking Banff and Lake Louise, ushering in the era of car-based tourism.

**1928** A log cabin is built at the site of today's Sunshine Village as a stopover for horse trekkers.

**1936** Temple Lodge is built across the Bow Valley from Lake Louise, the beginning of the Lake Louise ski resort's history.

**1941** The first rope tows are installed at Sunshine Village ski resort.

**1956** The Trans-Canada Hwy. 1 is completed through Banff and Yoho national parks.

**1961** Paving of the Icefields Parkway is completed.

**1985** Banff, Jasper, Yoho, and Kootenay national parks, along with four adjacent provincial parks, are declared a World Heritage Site by the United Nations Educational, Scientific and Cultural Organization (UNESCO).

**1990** Thanks to a joint agreement between local citizens and the federal and provincial governments, Banff becomes a self-governing municipality within the Province of Alberta, the only incorporated municipality within a Canadian national park.

**1998** The Delirium Dive area, a mecca for extreme skiers, is re-opened at Sunshine Village.

**1999** Parks Canada begins requiring hikers to travel in tight groups of four in high grizzly bear territory, especially around Moraine Lake during peak summer hiking season.

**2007** Banff's downtown core undergoes a redevelopment to replaced dated infrastructure, making it more pedestrian friendly.

# Toll-Free Numbers & Websites

### Airlines
**AIR CANADA**
☎ 888/247-2262
www.aircanada.ca
**ALASKA AIRLINES**
☎ 800/252-7522
www.alaskaair.com
**AMERICAN AIRLINES**
☎ 800/433-7300
www.aa.com
**BRITISH AIRWAYS**
☎ 800/247-9297
☎ 0870/850-9-850
in the U.K.
www.british-airways.com
**CONTINENTAL AIRLINES**
☎ 800/525-0280
www.continental.com
**DELTA AIR LINES**
☎ 800/221-1212
www.delta.com
**FRONTIER AIRLINES**
☎ 800/432-1359
www.frontierairlines.com

**NORTHWEST AIRLINES**
☎ 800/225-2525
www.nwa.com
**UNITED AIRLINES**
☎ 800/241-6522
www.united.com
**US AIRWAYS**
☎ 800/428-4322
www.usairways.com
**WESTJET**
☎ 888/937-8538
www.westjet.com

### Car-Rental Agencies
**ALAMO**
☎ 800/327-9633
www.goalamo.com
**AVIS**
☎ 800/331-1212
in the continental U.S.
☎ 800/TRY-AVIS
(879-2847) in Canada
www.avis.com

**BUDGET**
☎ 800/527-0700
www.budget.com
**DOLLAR**
☎ 800/800-4000
www.dollar.com
**ENTERPRISE**
☎ 800/325-8007
www.enterprise.com
**HERTZ**
☎ 800/654-3131
www.hertz.com
**NATIONAL**
☎ 800/CAR-RENT
(227-7368)
www.nationalcar.com
**THRIFTY**
☎ 800/367-2277
www.thrifty.com

## Major Hotel & Motel Chains

**BEST WESTERN INTERNATIONAL**
☎ 800/528-1234
www.bestwestern.com

**COMFORT INNS**
☎ 800/228-5150
www.hotelchoice.com

**DAYS INN**
☎ 800/325-2525
www.daysinn.com

**DELTA HOTELS & RESORTS**
☎ 877/814-7706
www.deltahotels.com

**FAIRMONT HOTELS**
☎ 800/257-7544
www.fairmont.com

**FOUR SEASONS**
☎ 800/819-5053
www.fourseasons.com

**HILTON HOTELS**
☎ 800/HILTONS (445-8667)
www.hilton.com

**HOLIDAY INN**
☎ 800/HOLIDAY (465-4329)
www.ichotelsgroup.com

**HOWARD JOHNSON**
☎ 800/654-2000
www.hojo.com

**HYATT HOTELS & RESORTS**
☎ 800/228-9000
www.hyatt.com

**MARRIOTT HOTELS**
☎ 800/228-9290
www.marriott.com

**RADISSON HOTELS INTERNATIONAL**
☎ 800/333-3333
www.radisson.com

**RITZ-CARLTON**
☎ 800/241-3333
www.ritzcarlton.com

**SHERATON HOTELS & RESORTS**
☎ 800/325-3535
www.sheraton.com

**WESTIN HOTELS & RESORTS**
☎ 800/937-8461
www.westin.com

# Index

See also Accommodations and Restaurant indexes, below.

# Photo **Credits**

p 1: © John E Marriott/All Canada Photos; p 4: © Craig Douce; p 5: © John Sylvester/All Canada Photos; p 6, bottom: © Darwin Wiggett/All Canada Photos; p 10, top: © Pictures Colour Library; p 11: © Ron Watts/All Canada Photos; p 14: © Courtesy of Fairmont Hotels & Resorts; p 15: © Miles Ertman/All Canada Photos; p 16, top: © Darwin Wiggett/All Canada Photos; p 16, bottom: © Pictures Colour Library; p 17: © John E Marriott/All Canada Photos; p 20, top: © John E Marriott/All Canada Photos; p 20, bottom: © Tom Nevesely/All Canada Photos; p 21: © Josh McCulloch/All Canada Photos; p 23: © John E Marriott/All Canada Photos; p 24: © Darwin Wiggett/All Canada Photos; p 25, top: © John E Marriott/All Canada Photos; p 26: © Miles Ertman/All Canada Photos; p 27: © Max Schoffel/patagoniatravelco. com; p 28: © Scott Dimond/All Canada Photos; p 30: © Kelly Funk/All Canada Photos; p 31: © John E Marriott/All Canada Photos; p 33: © Mike Grandmaison/All Canada Photos; p 35: © Michael Wheatley/All Canada Photos; p 39: © John E Marriott/All Canada Photos; p 42, top: © Courtesy of Fairmont Hotels & Resorts; p 42, bottom: © Craig Douce; p 43: © Ryan Creary/All Canada Photos; p 45: © Kurt Werby/All Canada Photos; p 46: © Bruce Obee/All Canada Photos; p 46: © Josh McCulloch/All Canada Photos; p 47: © John E Marriott/All Canada Photos; p 48: © Don Johnston/All Canada Photos; p 49: © Brad Wrobleski/All Canada Photos; p 51: © Max Schoffel/patagoniatravelco.com; p 54, top: © Spencer Francey; p 55: © Leslie Davis performs as Phaedra in Benjamin Britten's Phaedra. Photo Don Lee, courtesy of the Banff Centre; p 57: © Darwin Wiggett/All Canada Photos; p 59: © Ryan Creary/All Canada Photos; p 62: © Courtesy of Fairmont Hotels & Resorts; p 63: © Randy Lincks/All Canada Photos; p 65: © John E Marriott/All Canada Photos; p 66, bottom: © Darwin Wiggett/All Canada Photos; p 67: © Darwin Wiggett/All Canada Photos; p 69: © Courtesy: Maple Leaf Grill & Lounge; p 71, top: © Courtesy of Fairmont Hotels & Resorts; p 71, bottom: © The Rimrock Resort Hotel; p 74: © Heather McCoy; p 75: © Max Schoffel/patagonia-travelco.com; p 77: © Courtesy of Banff Lodging Co.; p 79: © Courtesy of Fairmont Hotels & Resorts; p 80: © Courtesy of Fairmont Hotels & Resorts; p 81: © Courtesy of Banff Lodging Co.; p 82, top: © Courtesy: Post Hotel & Spa; p 82, bottom: © The Rimrock Resort Hotel; p 83: © Spencer Francey; p 86: © Max Schoffel/patagoniatravelco.com; p 87: © Max Schoffel/patagoniatravelco.com; p 88, bottom: © Max Schoffel/patagoniatravelco.com; p 89: © The Festival Dance ensemble in Peggy Baker's "Julio Luomo" Photo: Donald Lee, Courtesy of The Banff Centre; p 90: © Aurora Nightclub; p 91: © Josh McCulloch/All Canada Photos; p 93, bottom: © Roy Ooms/All Canada Photos; p 94: © Darwin Wiggett/All Canada Photos; p 96: © Max Schoffel/patagoniatravelco.com; p 97, top: © Max Schoffel/patagonia-travelco.com; p 99: © John E Marriott/All Canada Photos; p 100, bottom: © Pictures Colour Library - PCL; p 101: © Darwin Wiggett/All Canada Photos; p 102: © Sam Chrysanthou/All Canada Photos; p 104: © Max Schoffel/patagoniatravelco.com; p 105, bottom: © Darwin Wiggett/All Canada Photos; p 107: © Tyler Mallory/Alamy; p 108: © Josh McCulloch/All Canada Photos; p 109: © Darwin Wiggett/All Canada Photos; p 111, top: © Kicking Horse Mountain Resort/McPhoto; p 111, bottom: © Michael Melford/Getty Images; p 114: © Paul Holscher; p 115: © Pictures Colour Library - PCL; p 117, bottom: © John E Marriott/All Canada Photos; p 118: © Barrett & MacKay/All Canada Photos; p 119, bottom: © Calgary Stampede; p 119, top: © Courtesy River Café; p 121: © Brownstock Inc./Alamy; p 132, bottom: © Courtesy Rocky Mountain Ski Lodge; p 133: © Max Schoffel/patagoniatravelco.com; p 135: © Courtesy Horsethief Creek Pub/Charlene Fuller; p 136, top: © Courtesy Kicking Horse Lodge; p 136, bottom: © Courtesy of Cathedral Mountain Lodge; p 137, top: © Courtesy of Canadian Rocky Mountain Resorts; p 137, bottom: © Copper Horse Lodge; p 138: © Don Gaynor; p 139: © John E Marriott/All Canada Photos; p 142: © Max Schoffel/patagoniatravelco.com; p 144, top: © John E Marriott/All Canada Photos; p 146, top: © Miles Ertman/All Canada Photos; p 147: © John E Marriott/All Canada Photos; p 148, top: © Josh McCulloch/All Canada Photos; p 148, bottom: © John E Marriott/All Canada Photos; p 149: © Michael Wheatley/All Canada Photos; p 151: © John E Marriott/All Canada Photos; p 152, top: © Kurt Werby/All Canada Photos; p 152, bottom: © Craig Douce; p 153: © John E Marriott/All Canada Photos; p 154, top: © Chris Cheadle/All Canada Photos; p 155: © Spencer Francey; p 157: © Ryan Creary/All Canada Photos; p 158: © Max Schoffel/patagoniatravelco. com; p 159: © Craig Douce; p 160: © Ryan Creary/All Canada Photos